The Renaissance

A Captivating Guide to a Remarkable Period in European History, Including Stories of People Such as Galileo Galilei, Michelangelo, Copernicus, Shakespeare, and Leonardo da Vinci

© Copyright 2019

All Rights Reserved. No part of this book may be reproduced in any form without permission in writing from the author. Reviewers may quote brief passages in reviews.

Disclaimer: No part of this publication may be reproduced or transmitted in any form or by any means, mechanical or electronic, including photocopying or recording, or by any information storage and retrieval system, or transmitted by email without permission in writing from the publisher.

While all attempts have been made to verify the information provided in this publication, neither the author nor the publisher assumes any responsibility for errors, omissions or contrary interpretations of the subject matter herein.

This book is for entertainment purposes only. The views expressed are those of the author alone, and should not be taken as expert instruction or commands. The reader is responsible for his or her own actions.

Adherence to all applicable laws and regulations, including international, federal, state and local laws governing professional licensing, business practices, advertising and all other aspects of doing business in the US, Canada, UK or any other jurisdiction is the sole responsibility of the purchaser or reader.

Neither the author nor the publisher assumes any responsibility or liability whatsoever on the behalf of the purchaser or reader of these materials. Any perceived slight of any individual or organization is purely unintentional.

Free Bonus from Captivating History (Available for a Limited time)

Hi History Lovers!

Now you have a chance to join our exclusive history list so you can get your first history ebook for free as well as discounts and a potential to get more history books for free! Simply visit the link below to join.

Captivatinghistory.com/ebook

Also, make sure to follow us on Facebook, Twitter and Youtube by searching for Captivating History.

Contents

INTRODUCTION 1

CHAPTER 1 – A BRIEF LOOK AT PRE-RENAISSANCE EUROPE 3

CHAPTER 2 – THE BLACK DEATH 7

CHAPTER 3 – THE ITALIAN RENAISSANCE 12

CHAPTER 4 – THE FALL OF CONSTANTINOPLE 16

CHAPTER 5 – THE PRINTING PRESS 20

CHAPTER 6 – LITERATURE OF THE 15TH CENTURY 23

CHAPTER 7 – THE NEW EDUCATION 28

CHAPTER 8 – THE MEDICIS OF FLORENCE AND FRANCE 33

CHAPTER 9 – THE DUTCH AND FLEMISH PAINTING REVOLUTION 37

CHAPTER 10 – LEONARDO DA VINCI 41

CHAPTER 11 – MICHELANGELO 44

CHAPTER 12 – COPERNICUS 48

- **CHAPTER 13 – THE REFORMATION** 51
- **CHAPTER 14 – THE SPANISH INQUISITION AND RENAISSANCE** 55
- **CHAPTER 15 – FRANCE AND THE WARS OF RELIGION** 59
- **CHAPTER 16 – ARTS AND POLITICS ACROSS RENAISSANCE EUROPE** 64
- **CHAPTER 17 – THE AGE OF DISCOVERY** 68
- **CHAPTER 18 – WOMEN'S EDUCATION** 73
- **CHAPTER 19 – GALILEO GALILEI** 77
- **CHAPTER 20 – ENGLISH RENAISSANCE UNDER THE TUDORS** 81
- **CHAPTER 21 – SHAKESPEARE, LULLY, AND THE NEW ART** 86
- **CHAPTER 22 – SEERS AND PROPHETS** 91
- **CHAPTER 23 – THE MEDICAL RENAISSANCE** 97
- **CHAPTER 24 – THE PERSECUTED INTELLECTUALS** ... 102
- **CHAPTER 25 – IN THE YEARS FOLLOWING THE RENAISSANCE** 105
- **REFERENCES** 107

Introduction

After the decline of the Roman Empire, huge populations of Europeans were suddenly left without the leadership, money, and political structure that had defined their culture for centuries. From the British Isles to Romania, right back to Rome itself, everything had changed—Europe was experiencing the Dark Ages.

This period of the Middle Ages in Europe was characterized by small tribal kingdoms, illiteracy, and the deterioration of science, math, philosophy, and art in education and wider culture. Ancient communities of Celts and Germanic tribes regained the strength they'd lost under the oppressive regime of the Roman Empire, while fractured Italy struggled to right itself and flush out the varied foreign rulers who had claimed principalities for themselves.

By the 11th century, Italy had reformed itself as the Kingdom of Italy, joining together with the Germanic nations of the north to become the Holy Roman Empire. The Papacy regained its former power over Christian Europe, while integrated local economies were able once more to create infrastructures capable of supporting international trade, military pursuits, and taxation. Once more in possession of strong roads, improved health, and access to food and shelter, people had the strength they needed to pursue higher arts and learning.

"Renaissance" is the French word for "rebirth," which is given to the period of time between the 14th and 17th centuries in Europe when there was a marked resurgence in classical art, education, philosophy, architecture, and natural sciences. Once more, the former Roman territories embraced the writings of ancient Greeks and Romans, and the idea of humanism. This rebirth marks the end of the Dark Ages and the beginning of the long march toward modernity.

In those precious centuries, astronomers redefined the way we view our place in the solar system and the universe. Writers and scholars gave us new ways of thinking about the human condition, the self, and the community. Artists found new methods of expression, and architects used classical pieces in their contemporary churches, palaces, and public buildings. Science leaped forward, once more able to match the level of Arab and Muslim intellectuals in terms of math and experimental philosophies.

At its heart, the Renaissance marked a widespread stability that Europe had not known for centuries, coupled with an inevitable desire of people everywhere to learn and express themselves. Education and economic stability transformed Europe into a beacon of high culture that eventually led to the Enlightenment and the Modern Age as we know it.

Chapter 1 – A Brief Look at Pre-Renaissance Europe

The Roman Empire, under the leadership of dozens of Caesars who answered to a democratically elected Senate back in Rome, colonized and occupied Europe, North Africa, and the Near East from about 200 BCE to the end of the 5th century CE.

During this intensive span of colonization, Rome rigorously oppressed local culture in favor of its own style of civilization. Believing that they were bringing a superior form of societal organization to the uncultured tribes around them, Rome was ruthless when it came to transforming the lands it conquered. Infrastructure was the first issue Caesar's soldiers dealt with once a region or small kingdom came under their control. Roads were constructed to connect military outposts and community centers, while walls went up to keep out unfriendly locals.

People throughout the empire lost touch with their cultural roots thanks to the inundation of Roman education and trade. What they gained was contemporary philosophy and literature, new political ideas, food, and supplies from a much larger region. The Roman stamp on Europe could—and sometimes still can—be physically seen in the forms of paving, fortified stone walls and forts, bridges like the Pont du Gard in France, libraries like the one still standing in Selçuk, Turkey, and public works like the Imperial Baths of Trier in Germany. Structures were strong, grand, and unlike anything the landscape or its people had seen before.

Life became very different under the rule of the Roman Empire, but their rule wouldn't last forever. Rome had spread itself very thinly across a massive expanse of land, and its enemies eventually gained a foothold. Under the leadership of Odoacer, Germanic tribes of the northern regions swept in and wrested control of all Italy from Emperor Romulus Augustulus. After several decades of struggling to maintain law and trade, most Roman colonies found themselves completely cut off from their long-time center of culture. There were no more wine, fruit, silk, or spices, and over time, there was an extreme dip in the level of literacy and higher education.

Multiple cultural groups reemerged in the absence of their central ruler, usually in support of powerful local families. Nearly three centuries after the fall of Rome, Emperor Charles le Magne (Charles the Great, modernized as Charlemagne) emerged as the leader of the Franks, while independent Viking raiders took over large sections of Britain and northwestern Europe. The remaining eastern collection of Roman colonies were still tightly interwoven, but they evolved into the Byzantine Empire, where Greek was the common language. The Byzantines were focused on maintaining the trade routes between Eastern Europe, North Africa, and Asia, which resulted in a rich and powerful culture centered in Constantinople.

Muslim caliphates conquered the former Roman regions in Egypt, Palestine, Syria, and Mesopotamia, reconstructing these places from weakly Christian centers into devoted Muslim societies. Modern Portugal and Spain were also heavily invaded by Muslim armies while simultaneously developing strong Christian communities within the Iberian Peninsula. It was an uncomfortable mixture that would only become more troublesome as the centuries of coexistence wore on.

The most defining political feature of Europe in this period was the emergence of dozens of small kingdoms, including that of Germany, Bohemia, Burgundy, the Franks, and Italy. In the latter half of the 10th century, many of these small realms were politically bound together under the newly emerged Holy Roman Empire. In the year 800 CE, Pope Leo III granted the title of Emperor to Frankish King Charles, thus beginning the secondary wave of Romanization of Western Europe. Some historians consider this consolidation the beginning of the Renaissance, or at least a separate and brief period of Roman revival in the west. The century following King Charles' crowning is known as the Carolingian Renaissance.

Indeed, Emperor Charlemagne's rule began 800 years of international accord under the umbrella of the Holy Roman Empire, which certainly played a large role in the reconnection of Western and Eastern Europe. The kingdoms were connected not only by trade and migration but by their shared belief in the Catholic Church. By concentrating on their alignment with the Church and its pope, European kingdoms grew larger, more powerful, and more prosperous. By requiring tithes—that is, mandatory donations—the Church became the central power in all Christian Europe. And monarchs, by pledging their sword and a portion of their own collected taxes to the pope, aligned themselves with this power.

Since their early Roman conquerors had brought Christianity with them near the end of the Classic Roman Period, most former colonies held tightly to the teachings of Christianity. Italy, the Franks, Germany, and various Spanish kingdoms were the biggest early supporters of Catholicism. Various realms within the British Isles remained aligned with the ideals and teachings of the Catholic Church, following in the footsteps of their families who proudly traced their lineage back to Rome. Pictland—or Scotland, to the modern ear—and Wales held tightly to their non-Roman, Celtic roots. That left most of England to the Christians, centered in the

Kingdoms of Mercia, Northumbria, and Wessex. Physically isolated from the regeneration of the rest of Europe, these islands suffered heavily from increasing Viking attacks in the centuries following the fall of Rome. In dealing with local challenges such as invaders, extreme difficulty in transportation, and war between themselves, English kingdoms and their close Celtic neighbors fell greatly behind mainland Europe.

Just prior to what is considered the true Renaissance, Europe's many kingdoms were in a state of constant vigilance between one another, and in constant vigilance of non-Christians among themselves. Borders had spread as large as politically possible without cultural and regional consolidation.

Like the French poet Alain de Lille wrote in the 12th century, "Mille viae ducunt homines per saecula Romam." That is, "A thousand roads lead men forever to Rome." De Lille may have been alive long after the fall of the Roman Empire, but he makes it clear that the influence of the world's most far-reaching cultural epicenter was anything but forgotten by its former colonies. Much of Western Europe lauded their connection to the original Roman colonial body and yearned for a return to what they viewed as the very height of culture and civilization. It would be 800 years before Europe's intellectuals considered themselves back on par with the philosophers, scientists, and artists of classical Rome.

Chapter 2 – The Black Death

Before the fog of the Dark Ages could clear sufficiently for Europe to embrace the Renaissance, the people had to throw off the shackles of a very debilitating part of their existence: the Black Death.

At a time far before antibiotics, before vaccines, and before humans even properly understood what caused sickness, one of the most persistent forms of illness was the plague. Alternatively called the Black Plague, or the Black Death, the illness claimed the lives of people young and old, rich and poor, healthy or weak, from the British Isles to the Black Sea and beyond. It is estimated to have killed up to 200 million people in Eurasia. The most devastating time period for contracting the Black Death was in the 14th century, but the disease returned to most capital cities every summer until finally winding down in the 18th century and coming to a stop in the 19th century.

Plague, still extant in some parts of the world today, is a quick-developing bacterial infection of the body's lymph nodes. Usually passed from infected animals to humans via fleas, the Black Death was so called because the affected lymph nodes turned black, signaling the onset of the disease. What followed were intense flu-like symptoms, high fever, and vomiting of blood. Those infected often died just days after black lumps first appeared in their armpits or groin.

Mid-14th-century Italy was struck with the worst pandemic yet. With people dying in multitudes every day, corpses burning in piles of hundreds at a time, and criminals freed from prison if they promised to help clear the bodies, society lost its sense of propriety, to say the least. People felt like the end of the world was at hand, and that no matter what measures they took to protect themselves against the illness, they would eventually succumb to the Black Death. Pope Clement VI ordered the fires of Avignon lit twenty-four hours a day in an effort to keep up with the bodies and burn away the disease. He allowed no one near him, giving orders from a distance.

Many people assumed they would die. In a panic, Christians tried to mend their souls and prepare them to meet their maker. To facilitate this preparation, the Brotherhood of the Flagellants appeared in Hungary and Germany. The group, comprised of all manner of people, began public self-punishment ceremonies in which they expunged themselves of sin and welcomed others to join in with prayers, supplications, and self-flagellation with barbed whips. The Brotherhood traveled from city to city, gathering more members and inciting hysteria amongst the peasantry, as well as religious clerics and even noble men and women. Their numbers reached the thousands, and the group split to travel north and south across Europe. The hysteria reached far and wide, out of control even of the pope, until the deaths from the plague began to slow. Then, the mania took a new form.

It was called the St. John's Dance, in which the pious joined hands, screeching and spasmodically dancing for hours upon hours, appearing neither to hear nor see the reality around them. After falling down from exhaustion, the dancers suffered from extreme sickness for a time before recovering to normalcy and eventually returning to the dance. When focused, the dancers told onlookers that they'd seen wonderfully spiritual hallucinations, such as the skies of heaven opening up. Thousands gathered to dance in German cities before the craze moved into Belgium and France. For some, the hysterical throes of passion moved them to undress and engage in sexual acts with one another. In the midst of the manic crowds, no behavior was out of sorts.

Others, terrified of the plague at its height but not swept up in the dancing hysteria, committed suicide to save themselves the pain. While the madness progressed, no clear solution could be found. The most respected theory during the 1400s concerning the contraction of the plague was that the infections were a result of having displeased God. Those who were suffering pleaded with priests to bless them and restore their reputation with God, while educated priests and monks looked frantically to their little knowledge of astronomy to try to understand what was happening. After the deaths of more than 10,000 people in Florence, metalsmith Lorenzo Ghiberti was commissioned to build a set of magnificent bronze doors to the Florence Baptistery as a plea to God to spare the city from more plague. His bronze panels, crafted intricately to depict scenes from the New Testament, were immediately considered a masterpiece. Michelangelo later referred to them as the Gates of Paradise.

As beautiful as the bronze panels of the great doors were, the plague continued to ravage Florence and the rest of Europe. Eventually, scientists dropped the theory that God was punishing the sick and proposed that the illness was passed through the air in foul-smelling clouds. Known as the miasma theory, the belief in dangerous odors led medical practitioners to try to combat the spread of the plague by introducing strong scents into their clothing and living spaces. Vinegar was one of the most popular remedies, splashed liberally on clothing and furniture, and rubbed into the skin of those who hoped to stay healthy.

For centuries, the cure to the plague was considered the surrounding of one's self with pleasing fragrances. Various oils, powders, and perfumes were concocted to serve this exact purpose. Soap, unfortunately, though it would have proven much more beneficial, did not come into common use until the 19th century. Physician Nostredame—whose name is usually Latinized into Nostradamus—created rose pills to help battle the sickness. Crafted from rose hips, these pills offered supplemental vitamin C to help strengthen the body's immune system, but there were no real medical breakthroughs to ease Europe's constant bacterial foe.

The forward momentum of the Republic of Florence hit a metaphorical wall during the mid-14th century when it was hit by the Black Death. The plague was a constant threat to all Europeans in the Middle Ages, and it regularly worked its way through every urban community. People with means—such as petty kings and their families—would usually make an effort to leave crowded cities during the hot summer months when the disease was most rampant. By the 1450s, however, there was no outrunning the Black Death, which wiped out about one-third of the entire population of Europe. It was a century of sickness and poverty that impacted every class and country, but the Renaissance wouldn't be put off any longer. Ironically, the mass death suffered by Italy and its neighbors served to further inspire the emergence of a culture of higher learning and expression.

In the 17th century, Antonio Medici of Florence took it upon himself to collect as many recipes to combat the plague as he could. These recipes contained mostly common food items such as garlic, walnuts, herbs, wine, and figs, but other considerably less appetizing items were meant to be mixed and applied to the body as salves. The recipes suggest mixing substances such as red dirt, sulfur, arsenic, Palestine incense, mercury, copper, and blacksmith's water (water used to quench and cool hot metal) to create medallions or fragrant sachets to wear defensively. The remedies that naturally repelled fleas and animals, such as garlic, may have had some luck with the bubonic plague, but once the disease mutated to pass from human to human, any advantage from such recipes was lost.

To help the sick, city leaders in heavily affected plague cities like Florence, Venice, and Paris hired plague doctors. These doctors took up residence in their host community and visited plague victims, ostensibly to ease their suffering and potentially offer a cure. In truth, however, plague doctors were usually not even trained as physicians. They had no idea what to do for patients and therefore were most useful in recording statistical data, such as the number of people infected and how many survived or died. In the worst plague seasons, contracted doctors often died alongside the patients or simply ran away.

Of the very limited abilities a plague doctor possessed, bloodletting and leech application were the most professional. Neither practice was useful to patients healthy or otherwise, of course, but they were regularly used even by trained physicians. For the time being, the importance of the flow of blood through the veins was the most sophisticated piece of information anyone had about the body. Medicine as an industry was only just coming into its own, and when the plague slowed its cull, the polymaths of the Renaissance would make leaps and bounds toward a more complete and useful understanding of human health. Philosophy would also take root once more, as the educated people of the continent found themselves in generally good health and wealthy enough to explore the meaning of life in a variety of ways.

Chapter 3 – The Italian Renaissance

Where the Roman Empire was first conceived, so its Renaissance also began—in Italy. Ancient trade routes had not only been recovered and maintained, but new ones had solidified between the independent Italian kingdoms, Mediterranean ports, and even Baltic ports at the northern edge of Europe. The leader of the pack was Florence, located midway between Rome and Milan.

Formerly a small community overshadowed first by Rome and then by Pisa to the west, Florence sits astride the Arno River in the northern section of Italy. Flowing south and then westward from Mount Falterona, the Arno crosses Florence, Empoli, and Pisa, naturally facilitating the transportation of goods and people all the way to the Tyrrhenian Sea on Italy's west coast.

As early as the 13th century, Florence was an international trading hub and home to an estimated 80,000 people. Merchants made regular visits to the city to buy or sell goods from across Europe and parts of Asia. Florence itself dealt mostly in wool (imported from England then cleaned, carded, spun, and dyed) and home-grown silks cultivated by mostly female workers.

Business was so good that the city was able to produce a fortune in gold coins, known as florins. It was among the few international currencies that emerged after the height of the Roman Empire and Persia, both currencies having been gone for over 500 years. The gold florin became the international standard currency, with Florentine banks spreading out along trade routes. At home, bankers created a foreign exchange market. As citizens of the financial center of Europe, Florentines learned to use advanced bookkeeping strategies and track stock investments.

The middle class grew alongside the new finance industry, creating a rare overflow of wealth among some families despite their lack of connections to the ruling monarch. The result of this financial freedom on the younger generations was a desire to immerse themselves in arts, philosophy, and natural sciences. Less burdened by constant labor, people looked to personal expression, specifically in the form of painting, glassworks, architecture, and writing.

Philosophy took an important role in the vibrant new city of Florence and surrounding urban centers, and Francesco Petrarca, more widely known as Petrarch, embraced it wholeheartedly. Born in Arezzo, Italy in 1304, Petrarch traveled extensively throughout Italy and France, finding his most fulfilling inspiration in the ruins of Rome. His writings are considered one of history's first collections of humanist philosophy—that is, displaying faith in human beings to establish right from wrong and accomplish their goals through learning. Humanism itself has evolved into various factions, but it's clear that Petrarch and his fellow Christian humanists intended to work within the doctrine of the Catholic Church. Petrarch himself hoped for a renewal of the Roman papacy after a long stretch of papal vacancy in Italy due to a schism within the Church itself.

Petrarch's most famous work is a collection of poems styled as letters to a love interest named Laura. Though Laura was likely an idealized and entirely fictional character, the deeply philosophical and intelligent way Petrarch described his emotions and his world in those letters captured the hearts of many readers. For his contributions to literature and diplomacy, Petrarch was crowned a poet in Rome, complete with a wreath of laurels. Paris offered him the same honor, but his first loyalties were to the lost civilization of his forebearers.

> Love is the crowning grace of humanity, the holiest right of the soul, the golden link which binds us to duty and truth, the redeeming principle that chiefly reconciles the heart to life and is prophetic of eternal good. (Petrarch, as quoted in *Notable Thoughts About Women: A Literary Mosaic* by Maturin Murray Ballou.)

While Petrarch theorized about how to combine humanism with Christianity, his contemporaries made a more physical impact on Florence and Italy as a whole. Giotto di Bondone was one such Florentine. Like Petrarch and the majority of his contemporaries, Giotto was a Christian man in favor of a rebirth of the Catholic Church and the arts, literature, and philosophy he believed it stood for. A wonderful painter, Giotto's works include *The Life of the Virgin* and *The Life of Christ* on the ceiling of Arena Chapel in Padua, northern Italy.

In 1334, Giotto was chosen to design the bell tower of the Florence Cathedral and is credited with the frescos of many churches during that era. His style was natural, moving away from the stiff and highly structured Byzantine styles of the time. The cathedral itself is considered by some historians to be the first architectural feat of the Renaissance. Built with bricks, which had fallen out of favor, and featuring an immense dome reminiscent of the Roman Pantheon, the Florence Cathedral is indeed a building out of its own time. Its builders used concrete building blocks in place of stone, reinforcing the dome with a series of internal ribs. Outstandingly, the Florence Cathedral was begun in 1296 and was not completed until 1436. It remains a major part of the city, standing as a testament to the return to classic Roman art, architecture, and Christian faith.

Florence's population was reduced by up to half during the 1400s, which meant far fewer workers available to process wool or silk or tend the banks and stock market. The arts suffered for several decades, but a few dedicated craftsmen turned the death and decay around them into artworks that still awe the world today. Francisco Traini's "Triumph of Death" is one such painting, in which a collection of well-to-do people stand before three filled coffins. Each corpse wears a set of clothing depicting them as a ruler, a clergy member, and a pauper. Traini is showing his audience that death is the great equalizer.

The plague slowed down the stylistic changes in artworks and buildings and put a severe strain on the financial industry in Florence, but it did not wipe out the philosophy and desire of so many to return to classic Roman ideals. When the major outbursts of sickness passed and the Black Death returned to its periodical visits, Florence and Italy stood ready to race forward into the future. Events in other parts of the world significantly impacted that momentum, particularly the influx of refugees fleeing the former great city of Constantinople.

Chapter 4 – The Fall of Constantinople

The infamous fortress city of Byzantium dates back to the 7th century BCE when it was established by colonial Greeks in what is now Turkey. The city sits straddling the wide Bosporus Strait and facing the Sea of Marmara to the south, looking northward to the Black Sea. The perfect location for sea transit and trade, the city blossomed immediately and swelled to 400,000 people during the Early Middle Ages.

For one thousand years, the city served as a capital city for the Greeks, the Romans, the Byzantines, and then the Ottomans. In 324 CE, Roman Emperor Constantine I captured and rebranded the city as his namesake, declaring it the center of the Christian world. In the Dark Ages, it was also the largest European city with the highest population of wealthy nobles—the precursor to 14th-century Florence.

The city was home to a large university and libraries that boasted various ancient texts, including remnants from the sacked Library of Alexandria in Egypt. Under the leadership of Constantine, former Byzantium was outfitted with a retaining wall that ran the full circumference of the city, even along the waterfronts. Further walls and a moat were added over the centuries until Constantinople was the most fortified city in Europe.

In the 15th century, Constantinople was nearly all that remained of the Byzantine Empire; it stood defiantly in the middle of the widespread Ottoman Empire. Under increasing pressure and attacks from the Ottomans, Byzantine Europe had crumbled slowly over the preceding decades. Barely a century and a half old, the Ottoman Empire took relatively swift control of Eastern Europe during the early Renaissance. Constantinople was under constant attack from the Ottomans, but thanks to its superb reinforcements, it withstood siege after siege.

When the Ottoman throne changed hands in 1451, the new Sultan Mehmed II made it his personal mission to finally sack Constantinople and claim it for his Muslim empire. His task was not as impossible as it would have been in former years, since by that point, the fortress city's population had dwindled to 50,000 at most. Emperor Constantine XI had only partial control of the city and paid tribute to his Ottoman peer during times of peace. Knowing that the new sultan intended to strike, Constantine threatened to collaborate with Mehmed II's cousin to usurp the Ottoman throne. Mehmed was not intimidated.

In a last-ditch effort to protect his city-state, Emperor Constantine sent messengers to the rest of Christian Europe—Germany, France, Italy, and Aragon among them—asking for assistance. Only Venice heeded the call and sent ships full of soldiers to fight alongside the Byzantine emperor. Constantine's troops numbered 7,000, while Mehmed II's were estimated at 100,000. Desperate, Constantinople's able fighting men were drafted into the ranks, numbering about 30,000. They had 26 ships; Mehmed had a hundred more.

At the beginning of April 1453, the battle began. Ottoman forces ignored the impenetrable waterfront walls to the south in favor of a land attack from the west, bringing massive cannons with them. At sea, Mehmed's mariners planned to sail down the waterway into the heart of the city, known as the Golden Horn. Anticipating this move, defenders placed an immense chain across the mouth of the inlet so that no ships could cross it. The strategy worked for weeks, holding enemy ships at arm's length while the fortress walls held strong against cannon fire in the west. Even Mehmed's oversized cannons could not break through the multiple layers of the wall, and since they took three hours to reload, it was possible for sections of impacted stone to be repaired before the next hit. As it had countless times before, Constantinople proved itself the strongest fortress in all Europe.

Changing tactics, Sultan Mehmed II ordered his navy to dock their ships and carry them overland to the point in the river that lay behind the chain. At the time, the most common type of naval vessel was the dhow, a relatively small ship with crews of 12-30. This bold move was successful, and Emperor Constantine XI was forced to remove some of his western forces from the wall to the eastern coast. As defenses along the wall were significantly weakened, Mehmed's armies and cannons were eventually able to destroy a gated section of the fortifications. A second gated section farther north was destroyed soon after, requiring Constantine's western troops to split up and guard both heavily.

The attacking forces continued their siege over long days until finally they took one of the wall towers. The Byzantines fell back, and the city fell to its Ottoman enemies. The emperor was killed as his citizens and soldiers attempted to flee to the east, boarding their own ships and dodging enemy swords along the way. Any citizens remaining within the city were ruthlessly murdered, raped, or taken hostage as wives and slaves. Households were ransacked of valuables, churches were pillaged, and everything of any value was stolen outright or sold to the highest bidder.

An eyewitness' account of the sacking of Constantinople was published in *They Saw It Happen: An Anthology of Eyewitness' Accounts of Events in European History, 1450-1600*:

When Mehmed (II) saw the ravages, the destruction and the deserted houses and all that had perished and become ruins, then a great sadness took possession of him and he repented the pillage and all the destruction. Tears came to his eyes and sobbing he expressed his sadness. 'What a town this was! And we have allowed it to be destroyed'! His soul was full of sorrow. And in truth it was natural, so much did the horror of the situation exceed all limits.

Under the new ruler, Constantinople's new name was Istanbul. Ironically, given the new age of movable type printing, very few other records exist from the Ottoman conquest—but many scripts were yet to come. A great deal of the books taken from the siege would find their way back into Christian Europe, fueling the fiery will of the Renaissance even as the last vestiges of classical Rome lay in ruins.

Chapter 5 – The Printing Press

Late Middle Ages Europe was very different from today in terms of literacy for two main reasons: Most people couldn't afford higher education, and the work involved in creating a written pamphlet or book was incredible. Without easily obtainable literature or the understanding of how to read or reproduce it, the majority of Europeans living in the 14th century were illiterate and not particularly bothered about it. They had other things to do, such as care for crops and gardens, and ply their trades.

Woodblock printing had been in use since at least 200 CE, but these methods were very time consuming, involving the complete carving out of the written page on a block of wood before painting it carefully and stamping it onto fabric. The only other method for writing or drawing on canvas was to use a single handheld pen or brush—a fine system for producing a single draft but useless for making multiple copies. For these reasons, few books existed throughout Europe at the start of the Renaissance, mostly concerning religious themes. They were written on leather or parchment and bound with wood.

In the 14th century, the love of reading and writing had started to spread outward from Florence and Italy, igniting the imaginations of people throughout the continent. All the way in England, Geoffrey Chaucer wrote an epic collection of stories entitled *The Canterbury Tales*, while a book of verses from Welsh authors was published under the title *The Red Book of Hergest*. In France, *Le Menagerie de Paris*, which was written by an anonymous Frenchman and made available in print form by Baron Jerome Pichon in 1846, was a guidebook for newly-married women that provided tips on how to make conversation, run a household, and acquire the love of God and your husband. An anonymous Byzantine author published one of the world's first romance novels, *Belthandros and Chrysantza*. Without fail, each published work referenced Christianity or Islam, either directly or indirectly.

Most scripts at the time were written in Latin, firstly because it was the most widely-known language throughout Europe, and also because written scripts hadn't necessarily been developed to the same standard for languages like Anglo-Saxon, Flemish, Briton, or Old Norse. Turning your quill to a niche vernacular was considered not only rather vulgar, but largely a waste of time—after all, what was to be gained from the effort of writing if the work couldn't be read by one's peers, and only by a very small number of educated people in one region?

Everything changed when Chinese printing technology was adapted by Johannes Gutenberg of Mainz, Germany. Asian inventors were way ahead of their European counterparts when it came to publishing, with Bi Sheng having created movable type ceramic, metal, and clay printing as early as 1040 CE. However, Gutenberg improved upon the existing technologies in a way that revolutionized even Chinese printing methods.

An experienced goldsmith, Gutenberg experimented with coin-punching hand molds until he perfected his handmade metal alphabet. Each letter, number, and punctuation mark was crafted individually so that the pieces could be arranged uniquely in a frame, inked, pressed onto parchment or paper, and then dissembled and rearranged as necessary. There was no more need to carve slabs of wood in backward-facing print for each page; no need for paint or inferior inks to rub on the molds either. Gutenberg developed a stickier oil-based ink that didn't run and pool as much as earlier types of ink, making the process of pressing paper over the frame much simpler. It was a brand-new way for the writers and thinkers of Europe to publish bigger books in larger numbers. Literature had been given new life, and it boomed throughout the continent.

Philosophers, poets, and storytellers came out of the woodwork over the course of the next few centuries, changing literature from a rare commodity into the hot new hobby for upper-middle-class Europeans. It wasn't just artists who wanted to put their work onto parchment, either—some of the most prolific writers of the Renaissance were kings and queens. It was another plain throwback to the time of Rome's Caesars, as Julius Caesar and Marcus Aurelius had written many manuscripts on the art of diplomacy and war in the previous and early half of the millennium.

King James I of Scotland wrote of his own capture and imprisonment by the English in *The King's Quair*, published in 1406. Like much Christian literature of the time, it rhymed. Rene of Anjou, King of Naples, penned *The Mortification of Vain Pleasure* in 1455, followed by *The Book of the Love-Smitten Heart* in 1457.

The Byzantine rulers of the era were just as eager to make their literary mark on the world, though they usually chose to write in Greek. Manuscripts of the Byzantine Empire date back to the 11th century, but by the mid-1400s, the empire was in serious trouble and unable to focus on the arts. Nearly all that remained of the Byzantines was their capital city.

Chapter 6– Literature of the 15th Century

Literature proved itself an unstoppable force that brought ideas to every corner of Europe thanks to Gutenberg's innovative printing press.

When Constantinople fell to the sultan, many of the books that survived were works of Greek and Roman philosophy, as the sciences and math were swallowed up into the Ottoman culture. Some, however, were hidden or purchased and whisked away to Italy, France, Spain, and other kingdoms still under the Christian faith. Suddenly, there was an important influx of classic literature that circulated throughout Europe and inspired a new generation of printing press equipped authors.

There were two fundamental outcomes from this combination of classic scrolls, books, and printing technology. Firstly, news could be easily spread from region to region, keeping the literate informed about their neighbors and their own kingdoms; and secondly, the standardization of language itself became established. Thanks to Gutenberg and the secreted books of Constantinople, changes in culture and education swept through the continent. News, trade, alliances, and personal creativity were all affected.

Court messengers had once been required to remember the words of one message across vast distances before relaying what was hopefully a mostly correct paraphrase to the recipient. Unable to write or read notes, news was slow moving and simplistic to keep it error free. As education became more highly valued in the 14th and 15th centuries, of course, nobility could handwrite their own parchments and have messengers hand deliver them virtually anywhere. This worked as recipients were usually highly educated people who were taught to write and read the same—or a similar—dialect of one or two languages, but wider distances created problems of clear communication.

Even two people from the same kingdom could misunderstand each other since traffic only moved at the speed of a horse and each tiny community developed and used its own forms of slang, idioms, spelling, and grammar. Though messages themselves remained handwritten, the hundreds of books, pamphlets, and stories coming out of the printing presses of the continent were traveling alongside messengers, wanderers, families, and workers from place to place, bringing contemporary events and lifestyles to the attention of readers near and far. For the first time, literate people everywhere had the chance to learn about the people, cultures, and events around them—and to assimilate those isolated pieces of language into a universal form of English, Spanish, French, and every other major tongue.

Perhaps the sheer excitement of reading news and fictional stories motivated Europe to focus more on literary and classical education. From the top down, it was the continent's leaders, the wealthy and finally the upper middle classes who acquired literary, philosophical, and scientific knowledge from this point onward. As more people throughout Europe learned to read and write, more people became authors and readers themselves. With more perspectives than ever, literature grew in leaps and bounds, combining hyperlocal styles like the Briton epic poem and the French character handbook. Religion became less of a prime reason for writing, though it kept its place in the context of various fictional plots.

In England, Thomas Malory created a work of fiction based on one of the realm's most enduring figures: the legendary King Arthur. His two-volume book, *Le Morte D'Arthur*, was written in the Middle English of 1485. Because of the Norman conquest of England in 1066, Renaissance England's nobility spoke and wrote a language heavily influenced by contemporary French languages. Thanks to literature like the following (in which Arthur Pendragon pulls the holy sword from the stone), residents of the various English kingdoms found a common voice among one another that promoted nationalism and finally pieced together the English and French languages.

"Now assay," said Sir Ector unto Sir Kay.

And anon he pulled at the sword with all his might; but it would not be.

> "Now shall ye assay," said Sir Ector to Arthur. "I will well," said Arthur, and pulled it out easily. And therewithal Sir Ector knelt down to the earth, and Sir Kay.

"Alas," said Arthur, "my own dear father and brother, why kneel ye to me?"

> "Nay, nay, my lord Arthur, it is not so; I was never your father nor of your blood, but I wot well ye are of an' higher blood than I weened ye were."

> And then Sir Ector told him all, how he was betaken him for to nourish him, and by whose commandment, and by Merlin's deliverance.

Michel de Montaigne, a contemporary of Princess Margaret of Valois and a survivor of the Massacre of St. Bartholomew's Day during the French Wars of Religion, served the French Crown as a statesman and a humanist. Descended both from Roman Catholics and a Jewish family, de Montaigne was trusted on behalf of the French court and that of Navarre to perform diplomatic tasks. Montaigne's main contribution to the French Renaissance, however, was more on the literary bent.

Personally speaking, Montaigne lamented the state of French literature of his time, remarking in his own work how it delighted him to find some compelling passages among the French books he looked at in passing. He wanted more from his country's scholars and traveled extensively in the decade following the tragic massacre in Paris, in part seeking relief from his chronic health issues and writing detailed essays about his experiences. This form of writing was Montaigne's lasting contribution to French literature and modern writing throughout the Westernized world.

Spanish writers remained quite firmly attached to religious works, authoring philosophical and speculative interpretations of the Catholic gospels mostly until the latter part of the Renaissance. When they did embrace the full opportunities in fiction, they found a particular love of the romance novel. One of history's best-remembered authors, Miguel de Cervantes, created a timeless character in his 1605 book *Don Quixote de la Mancha*. The book was named for the romance-obsessed protagonist himself.

> This…gentleman…spent his times of leisure—which meant most of the year—reading books of chivalry with so much devotion and enthusiasm that he forgot almost completely about the hunt and even about the administration of his estate; and in his rash curiosity and folly he went so far as to sell acres of arable land in order to buy books of chivalry to read…

> With these words and phrases the poor gentleman lost his mind, and he spent sleepless nights trying to understand them and extract their meaning, which Aristotle himself, if he came back to life with only that purpose, would not have been able to decipher or understand.

Thanks to the outpouring of contemporary fiction throughout the European Renaissance, historians have a wide selection of literature from which to study and better understand the period. Through the countless poems, manuals of conduct, books of chivalry, romances, and adventure stories, Renaissance authors reveal a wide world of developing regional and international ties. Relationships between small kingdoms and their common leader, the Catholic Church, were in a constant state of flux as they stretched their political and economic legs and jostled for a prime position in world trade and land ownership.

Thanks to language standardization and renewed linguistic education, Europe started to feel like a much smaller place. Political boundaries stretched and new alliances were made that started to shape the European map into something we might recognize today.

Chapter 7 – The New Education

The formative philosophical theory underlying the evolution of education during the Renaissance was humanism. Initially meant to embody a study of human nature from the perspective that the Catholic Bible was an infallible truth, humanism split quickly into various factions. These factions included Stoic, Christian, Aristotelian, and eventually Secular Humanism. The most influential philosophies of the time were Christian-based humanist ideas, in which the Catholic Church and its aligned kingdoms were highly revered and outright indulged.

Another definitive philosophical school of the time is classified as Renaissance Platonism, a fresh look at works from classic Greek educator, Plato. His was a philosophy in sharp contrast to the more literal theory of humanism since Plato believed the mind and the spirit were greater than the physical self or one's literal surroundings.

Almost purely because of this Platonic revival in 14th-century Florence, higher education of subsequent centuries included Greek lessons that equipped students to read the source material. Alongside Latin, Greek was revered as an almost holy connection with the continent's ancient philosophers.

French scholar Michel de Montaigne (1533-1592) wrote extensively on the topic of education, at a time when scholasticism competed with secular forms of teachings throughout Europe. The following is from his book, *Of the Education of Children*:

> ...it is no hard matter to get children; but after they are born, then begins the trouble, solicitude, and care rightly to train, principle, and bring them up. The symptoms of their inclinations in that tender age are so obscure, and the promises so uncertain and fallacious, that it is very hard to establish any solid judgment or conjecture upon them.

As a renewed interest in the Greek and Roman classics spread from Italy westward, the method of teaching that usually accompanied such literature was scholasticism. This method consisted of three fundamental steps. First, the student must read a respected work, such as Aristotle's *Eudemian Ethics*. Second, he or she must read another work that criticizes the first. Third, the student must carefully consider each critical point and decide how to resolve any contradictions or disputes. The method came directly from clerical teaching methods, in which students of the Church were taught to defend religious dogma across scriptures.

Scholasticism didn't satisfy many tutors and professors of the mid- and late Renaissance, but it did provide a scholarly bridge into the contemporary study and practice of logic. Aristotle was considered the benchmark of philosophy for proponents of the method. Teaching developed independently thanks to the increased demand for tutors from 1400-1700, and pedagogy advanced alongside its subject matter. Science, for example, required its students not only to study the works of previous masters but to perform their own studies and research.

Educational curriculums that included multiple subjects were limited to the noble and wealthy citizens of Europe, while working classes taught their children a trade at home or sent them to become apprentices for in-demand professionals. Michel de Montaigne realized this and suggested that even if the poor could send their children to learn science and math, it would make no difference to the life of the student.

> ...science is a very great ornament, and a thing of marvellous use, especially in persons raised to that degree of fortune ... And, in truth, in persons of mean and low condition, it cannot perform its true and genuine office, being naturally more prompt to assist in the conduct of war, in the government of peoples, in negotiating the leagues and friendships of princes and foreign nations, than in forming a syllogism in logic, in pleading a process in law, or in prescribing a dose of pills in physic.

From about the 5th century in Europe, churches served as education centers, where literate monks would teach disciples to read and write Latin, as well as their chosen rules from the Catholic faith. Only the sons of wealthy landowners and nobility were able to attend school at all, which left most of the population illiterate and dependent on churches for religious interpretations. Crafts and trades fell under their own educational system, whereby skills and techniques in stonework, carpentry, livestock maintenance, and other professional skills were normally passed down from father to son in early apprenticeship. Outside of the family unit, apprenticeships were another potential form of education.

Though family trades and apprenticeships continued during the Renaissance, higher learning expanded into new universities and colleges that were built for the sole purpose of education. Dozens upon dozens of universities were established between the 14th and 17th centuries all across Europe, in cities such as Pisa, Avignon, Dublin, Firenze, Budapest, Bordeaux, and Edinburgh. Interestingly, given its distance from the center of the Renaissance, England established the Universities of Oxford, Northampton, and Cambridge as early as the 13th century. Many of these ancient educational facilities are still in existence today, heralded as forebearers of modern school systems.

Though Latin had continued to be taught in previous centuries, it now took on singular importance under the revised classical curriculum. At the age of five, sons of important and wealthy families were first introduced to the language of ancient Rome, embarking upon a ten-year journey with various professional authors, philosophers, scientists, and mathematicians to earn a well-rounded worldview. The student's native language was not a subject of study; tutors and families agreed that this was easily and naturally learned at home.

During the medieval period, education style, subject matter, and the age at which a child began lessons depended completely on a child's parents or guardians. There was no compulsory schooling, and indeed such legislation would have been fruitless since poor and middle-class families needed their children at home to help with farming, gardening, livestock care, and house maintenance. Older children worked with their parents or found jobs outside the house to contribute money or goods. When the Reformation took hold, Protestants sought to ensure that all young boys (and in some regions, girls too) were sent to school to become literate and learn how to read the Bible. Most European countries adopted mandatory schooling during the 16th and 17th centuries.

Once grammar, religion, and some history had been taught to a pupil, they moved onto university lessons that were organized according to a specific planet. The learned tutors, polymaths, and philosophers of the day ascribed common traits to the planets of their solar system—though they didn't all have quite the correct idea of what that was—and referred to each regularly in literature and science. University programs were largely comprised of seven schools of knowledge, known as the humanities or liberal arts. The moon represented grammar; Mercury represented logic; Venus represented rhetoric; the sun, music; Mars, arithmetic; Jupiter, geometry; and Saturn, astronomy and astrology. This basic curriculum was used right up into the early 20th century by tutors and professors teaching the children of aristocrats, royals, and other wealthy families.

Modern classes at public and private schools sometimes use an updated version of the scholasticism method, called the Harkness table. This provides a foundation of discourse between students and teachers throughout the learning process. In the last half-century, however, Latin and Greek courses have significantly gone out of fashion, to the point that only secondary students or private school students have access to classic curriculums. Most European schools offer Latin lessons as an option, with very few compulsory components.

Chapter 8 – The Medicis of Florence and France

Cosimo the Elder, active in the 15th century, is considered the founder of the powerful House of Medici. Thanks to the careful administrations of Cosimo, the family used its existing wealth and influence to patronize the humanities and support flourishing artists. Florence became a haven of education, philosophy, and artistic expression, while the Medicis cleverly solidified their power over the city-state. During the Renaissance, the family produced four Catholic popes and spread progeny throughout the various kingdoms of Europe by marrying into other important families. By the 16th century, Cosimo's most famous descendant, Catherine de' Medici, was queen of France.

In 1397, the well-off Medici family formed the Medici Bank and were an integral part of Florence's development as a world-class financial hub. Money lenders and savers of the Medici Bank used a new method of accounting, known now as the class double-entry bookkeeping system. Using what are now called general ledgers, the

Medicis and their contemporaries in Florence kept careful track of each florin from each individual account, using one side of the ledger for credit and the other for debt. This finely-tuned, careful method meant more reliable transactions for patrons of the bank. Ironically, the Medici name would not become synonymous with reliability.

Perhaps one reason for this is that the family were such high social climbers, and once they already had power of Florence and Tuscany, they purportedly began to invent grand stories of their ingenious and brave ancestors. They needn't have done so for Cosimo since it was largely the family patriarch who led them all to wealth and notoriety. Personally, Cosimo was quite humble, building a relatively modest estate for himself so as not to call too much attention to himself. After his death, the Medici family glorified him to no end, using that positive image to cement themselves into the future of Florence.

The family is famous because as the leaders of Florence they played a very important role in the Italian Renaissance. The money they invested in their city may have changed the world, thanks to the fact that successive generations of Medicis were faithful lovers of literature and art. Between them, the Medicis hired and supported Michelangelo, da Vinci, Botticelli, Raphael, and Brunelleschi, all of whom made lasting contributions to Renaissance art and science.

Alongside the return to classical Greek- and Roman-style philosophy and humanities was the rebirth of classical architecture. With more patronage from Medici city leaders and popes, architects of Venice and Florence were able to express the style of the times with the use of columns, arches, and domes that harkened back to ancient temples of the old gods. Cement and brick building resurged, allowing buildings greater heights and areas coupled with intrinsic strength. Symmetry and geometry ruled in the new style which soon made its way westward. Fine arts developed alongside construction arts, taking on a more realistic structure created with the emerging industry of oil painting.

Though Classicism was the first fountain from which contemporary artists drew their inspiration, artistic themes evolved over the course of the decades and centuries. Humanism, in art as in philosophy, was a commonly explored theme in much Renaissance art and architecture. Inundated by the spreading belief that humans were in control of their own destinies, artists started to capture realistic figures with individual facial expressions. Buildings were no longer just in praise to God, but a celebration of better understanding the physical sciences.

When Catherine de' Medici married French King Henry II and moved to Paris to await her role as queen of France, she brought a love of fine portraiture and exquisite furniture with her. She collected art, ivory sculptures, and books that no doubt occupied her during the years that her husband left her mostly to her own devices, preferring to deal with politics—and his mistress, Diane de Poitiers—on his own. Nevertheless, the couple came under extreme pressure to produce children once Henry's older brother died and left him heir to the throne. Catherine was forced to try absurd fertility methods that included mule urine and cow feces. In time, she became pregnant and gave birth to a son. In all, Catherine birthed ten children, six of whom survived childhood.

Other than producing children, Catherine de' Medici was allowed very little influence at the French court until her husband died in 1559. From the moment Henry II lay dying, Queen Catherine saw her opportunity to make up for lost time. She denied Diane de Poitiers access to the dying man, and once Henry was gone, she banished his former mistress from court and demanded Diane return the crown jewels she had been given by the former king. Though her son was old enough to rule on his own, he made a point of referencing his mother every time he addressed parliament or issued a proclamation. Catherine proudly stood by Francis II and made an international name for herself as the conniving woman behind the throne. She likely was not bothered.

Francis II died young, leaving Catherine de' Medici to rule as regent of France for her next oldest son, Charles IX. At the death of Charles, her grown son Henry III succeeded. Each of Catherine's sons loved and respected her, which meant that she had every bit of influence that she had lacked while her husband was alive. Unfortunately, during the reigns of her sons, Catherine faced extreme violence between the Catholics and Protestants in her kingdom. The queen tried to achieve a balance between the groups, but all attempts were unsuccessful, leading to the French Wars of Religion.

In 1587, when Catherine's former daughter-in-law was executed in Protestant England, the Catholic backlash gained momentum again and threatened to oust her and her son from the throne of France. Henry III was forced to hire a Swiss guard to protect him from the Catholic Guise family, relatives of the murdered Mary, Queen of Scots. The Guises seized much control of Paris, causing bloodshed between the king's followers and those of the Guises. Catherine died in 1589, shortly after learning that her son's men had murdered several Guise men.

Blamed ruthlessly for the bloodshed and political manipulation, Catherine was mourned by very few outside her own family. Less than a year later, Henry III was stabbed to death, bringing an end to the Valois Dynasty. None of Catherine's sons bore any heirs, effectively bringing the direct patriarchal line to an end.

Chapter 9 – The Dutch and Flemish Painting Revolution

Though oil painting would come to embody the bulk of artistic works of the European Renaissance, the use of such paints was not an immediate success. It wasn't until artists in the Netherlands were introduced to the innovative process of mixing colored pigments in vegetable oils that using such paints really took off. Before artists such as Jan van Eyck and Rogier van der Weyden made oil painting famous, painters would use their pigments directly on wet plaster or mix colors with quick-drying egg whites. By perfecting the use of linseed oil with their pigments, Dutch painters were able to create ultra-detailed realism that was otherwise unachievable.

The pigments they worked with were also becoming more sophisticated, and by the 17th century, several new colors joined the painter's palette, including Naples yellow, Carmine Lake, and smalt. Made from ground crystalline compounds, these colors were reddish-yellow, crimson, and powder blue, respectively. Artists obtained these and other pigments via trade merchants and either bought them mixed or used walnut or linseed oil to mix the paint themselves. Folding the crushed color pigments slowly into a small amount of oil produced a silky, thick, vibrant paint that blazed over the canvas.

Jan van Eyck was one of those talented early Dutch Renaissance painters who influenced the entire continent with his oil works. In the employ of John III, Duke of Bavaria-Straubing, van Eyck was already a master painter, sought after by art apprentices in and beyond The Hague. He assisted in revamping the immense local government buildings called the Binnenhof Palace. After the death of John III—AKA John the Pitiless, thanks to his habit of setting armies on family members and disobeying orders of the Church—van Eyck went to serve Philip the Good, Duke of Burgundy, in Bruges, Belgium. Exceptionally talented, van Eyck is responsible for the infamous *Arnolfini Portrait*.

Painted in 1434, the *Arnolfini Portrait* is a very early example of Renaissance style portraiture. It features stunningly realistic renderings of bright, vibrant fabrics, done in oil on oak. Famous both for being one of the first non-egg-based paintings and its incredible detail, the portrait reveals incredibly pale, exotic-seeming profiles of a contemporary man and his wife. They are dressed in what are probably their finest clothes, the young woman so heavily draped in a deep green gown that she has to hold the excess length up folded at her waist. The woman's dress is so finely worked that each crease and pleat is visible, while the man's sleeves show similar care and splendor. Tapestries and bedclothes in the background show more evidence of luxury, suggesting the portrait's sole purpose was to display the wealth and status of the couple. It has even been posited that the painting itself was done to record the marriage contract.

Holland's most lucrative painting commissions were split mostly between van Eyck and his peer, Rogier van der Weyden. In 1436, the latter was named Painter to the Town of Brussels. Like van Eyck, he mostly painted portraits and religious depictions, using oil-mixed paints to develop stunningly realistic textiles and features in his work. The likenesses of van der Weyden's subjects were perhaps a little better rendered than those of his contemporary; however, he has been criticized for beautifying the features of otherwise plain faces.

Der Weyden's painting, *Portrait of a Lady*, shows just how exacting a talented artist could be with slow-drying oil-based paints. Since oils took a much longer time to dry on canvas, wood, and other paint mediums than the yolk mixtures most artists used at the time, der Weyden taught himself how to delicately blend the wet paints together to create fine, realistic shading. *Portrait of a Lady* showcases this technique, with the painter's amazing rendition of a sheer headdress with clear fold marks over the subject's hair and face.

The near photorealism of some of der Weyden's and van Eyck's paintings was unprecedented in the European art scene, and their expertise and experiments with oils eventually diffused throughout the entire continent. By the end of the Renaissance, oil painting had become the norm for all fine portraitists and artists favored by the monarchy. Nearly 600 years later, the advancements made by that first handful of Dutch painters are still in use.

Joachim Patinir, a Flemish (from the Dutch-speaking portion of Belgium) painter born in 1480 took his predecessor's oil techniques to another level, using vibrant colors and shading techniques to step outside of traditional portraiture and biblical retellings. Patinir was the first successful Western European artist during the Renaissance period to establish landscape painting as a viable industry. His contemporaries, the German Albrecht Altdorfer and Italian Giorgione, produced some landscape works on their own during the same period. Patinir's works had the marked characteristic of featuring very small human figures, thereby solidifying the landscape itself as the focus. In many pieces, he would even have the people painted by other artists, while he dedicated himself to the trees, grasses, shrubs, and water features.

Patinir's landscapes established the modern norm for other paintings of similar types, in that they were largely divided into the foreground, mid-ground, and sky. The foregrounds are heavy in shades of brown, the mid-grounds are generally in shades of green, and the skies are painted in blue. His subjects were biblical figures, as that was overwhelmingly the style of the day—with the obvious exception being paid portraiture. He occasionally created works in the triptych style, in which three separate panels are used for one complete painting. Patinir's style was copied and further perfected by successive Dutch painters, including Pieter Bruegel the Elder and Pieter Aertsen.

The expressive paintwork of a multitude of highly talented Dutch and Flemish artists throughout the Renaissance laid the groundwork for technical advancements in shading, coloring, blending, and mixing paints, as well as oil and pigment; they also had a large hand in establishing landscapes and still lifes, styles that became in vogue throughout the continent. The discoveries made by these artists form much of the basis of modern painting techniques throughout Europe and the wider world.

Chapter 10 – Leonardo da Vinci

Certainly one of the best-known polymaths of all time, let alone the European Renaissance, was Leonardo da Vinci, who was patronized by none other than Lorenzo de' Medici, a descendant of Cosimo. Born outside of Florence to a peasant woman and a married nobleman, Leonardo's artistic strengths were his saving grace. A talented musician, artist, scientist, and engineer, the young illegitimate son of Piero da Vinci was employed under the Medici family as a painter and diplomat. He spent much of his time visiting nearby kingdoms and independent states as a representative of Florence and the Medicis, using his gifts of artworks to make peace and forge international friendships.

Long before da Vinci found fame as an artist and great thinker, he was a simple apprentice at the studio of Andrea del Verrocchio in Florence. Under Verrocchio, da Vinci learned a range of artistic methods, including how to work with stone and precious metals. His preferred method involved a paintbrush, and it would come to define him in hindsight. A constant student of the scientific method,

Leonardo's paintings were completed slowly and methodically, which is probably why he finished only a fraction of the artworks of his contemporaries.

Beginning his professional artistic career in the 1470s, Leonardo was a man who believed that art was an integral part of science, nature, and invention. Much as educated Europe had come to base their ideas and work on Latin literature, da Vinci used drawing as part of his creative and scientific process. An excellent example of the blended lines between art and science is Leonardo's *Vitruvian Man*. Drawn with ink on paper, this work depicts a bare human male form in two positions superimposed over one another. Around the figure, Leonardo wrote notes comparing the ideal structure of man to the architectural laws described by 1st-century BCE Roman architect, Vitruvius. Both the architect and his future follower used the human body to try to find a perfect geometrical symmetry that could be duplicated in artificial structures.

As a painter, Leonardo's most famous works include the *Mona Lisa* and *The Last Supper*, both of which are still known in almost any part of the world even now. Though only a few paintings may come to mind when we think of da Vinci, it was through painting that he earned his living and his reputation as a wonderful artist. His figures were neat and pretty, modern in terms of realism and quite recognizable as his own work. Outside of commissioned portraiture, da Vinci's paintings and sketches depicted biblical scenes that often included Jesus. Much of his work was relatively small, with the obvious exception of mural work. Even the *Mona Lisa* is just 77 x 53 centimeters (about 30 x 21 inches).

It is in the pages of da Vinci's many journals that we find the essence of the man. A cursory glance at over 13,000 pages of surviving sketches and notes shows how Leonardo often kept his records in backward cursive handwriting, written from right to left. Though this may seem quite puzzling, it is actually a common trait shared by left-handed people—of which Leonardo was one. Among the designs found scribbled in those notebooks are shoes for walking on water, a flying machine, a dive suit, parachutes, crossbow, and an anemometer, a device that measures the speed of wind.

He tended to sketch every device he imagined, laying it out geometrically as in an engineering blueprint. The pages also show his passion for fine art in the multiple human faces and drawings of birds in flight. Da Vinci was clearly very interested in anatomy as it related to the sciences of medicine and drawing, so much so that he used cadavers to teach himself the various parts of the body. Through the dissection of the dead, da Vinci came to better understand the forces that keep humans alive and those that take them from life.

Da Vinci wrote of an encounter he had with a man of about 100 years of age in a hospital in Florence. The old man told da Vinci that he felt perfectly fine and in good health, and that except for a general weakness, he really didn't feel any different than he had as a much younger man. "And thus, without any movement or sign of any mishap, he passed from this life. And I dissected him to see the cause of so sweet a death."

In his lifetime it is estimated that Leonardo da Vinci dissected at least thirty cadavers in hopes of learning the secrets of life and the building blocks of human anatomy. His notebooks are filled with what are some of the world's first medical illustrations, complete with personal notes describing the bits and pieces of each cadaver. These are still some of the most high-quality anatomical illustrations in the industry. Experts argue that it is perhaps for this that the great da Vinci should be remembered instead of merely for a little portrait of a mysterious woman.

Chapter 11 – Michelangelo

The 16th century brought yet another Italian polymath to the scene, this one by the name of Michelangelo di Lodovico Buonarroti Simoni. Known more simply as Michelangelo, this man could wield a pen, a paintbrush, and an architect's ruler with equal strength. Like the Medicis, Michelangelo's family gained their wealth as bankers in the 15th century, but eventually, their financial business failed and they moved outside of the city. After the death of his mother, young Michelangelo went to live with a nanny and her husband in the town of Settignano in Tuscany. There, in the shadow of his stonecutter father figure, the future builder and sculptor watched and learned the secrets of working with marble.

Though he became a talented artist in various media, Michelangelo worked with marble throughout his entire career and favored it considerably. Sent to a humanist school in Florence, the boy was uninterested in Latin grammar and ancient scrolls. He became apprenticed to Domenico Ghirlandaio, one of the artists called to paint the walls of the Sistine Chapel, at the age of thirteen. Only one year later, Ghirlandaio agreed to pay Michelangelo as an artist. As his work gained notoriety, Michelangelo moved up in the world quickly when Lorenzo de' Medici came to hire the two best students at Ghirlandaio's studio. Straightaway, at the tender age of 14, Michelangelo was whisked away to the Medici's neo-Platonic humanist academy.

Under Lorenzo's care, Michelangelo was given his own room at the palace, fine clothes, and a generous salary that most artists would never secure for themselves. At the new school, the young Michelangelo developed an ego that put him at odds with the other students. He felt that his work was superior to that of his peers, and his attitude resulted in a life-changing fistfight with one of the other boys at the academy. Michelangelo suffered a broken nose that healed crookedly. Humiliated at what he felt was a debilitating ugliness, the artist became even more passionate about producing perfection in his pieces.

After Lorenzo's death in 1494, Florence fell into political disarray. Evangelist Girolamo Savonarola incited hatred against the arts and in particular against the classical style works depicting male nudes. Savonarola held regular bonfires of the vanities in which he and his followers piled luxury items and artworks deemed inappropriate and set them alight. Priceless books, poems, and paintings were destroyed, along with mirrors, luxurious clothing, and anything considered vain, overtly sexual, or heretical in nature.

Michelangelo was conflicted at the onslaught of anti-classical rhetoric. He was a faithful Catholic but also an artist whose primary inspiration came from pagan Greek and ancient Roman works. Unsure what else to do, he left Florence and traveled to Venice for a time before finding a commission for angelic sculpture in Bologna. When the job was finished, he went back to Florence, poor and desperate to sell something quickly. It occurred to him that the money could be better found not in new works of art but in antiques—and so he used his talents to create beautiful classical style works that he could pass off as early Roman or Greek.

The first forgery Michelangelo produced was that of a sleeping marble cherub. Once the form was carved and perfected, the artist buried it in the dirt and probably employed various techniques to make the statue appear very old, at least 1,000 years in age. Satisfied, he brought it into an art dealer and found a buyer. The statue was purchased by an important Roman cardinal who immediately summoned Michelangelo to Rome for a meeting.

Understandably nervous, the artist asked if he could have the statue back if he returned the money. Cardinal Riario, however, declined the offer, explaining that he knew the cherub was a fake not because it didn't look old but because the pose was too modern. Michelangelo had put too much of his own perspective into the work to create a convincing forgery; instead of being punished, he was offered a commission. Cardinal Riario wanted a brand-new sculpture, of the artist's own choosing, for his collection.

Once more, Michelangelo's artistic personality landed him in trouble. He created a large likeness of the god Bacchus, Roman patron of wine, seemingly unbalanced and evidently inebriated. Again, the sculpture seemed at first glance to be a genuine piece of classical art, but the figure's lack of decorum seemed outright insulting to a patron of such standing. Riario refused to buy the statue. The artist sold it instead to Jacopo Galli, the cardinal's banker.

Despite the near-disaster of his work with *Bacchus*, Michelangelo's name was growing in fame. He received more and more commissions and started to visit the marble quarry personally to choose his stone. It was his next employer, however, who would choose the giant block from which he would form his most famous statue: *David*. *David* was no small feat, and Michelangelo agonized over every detail. Determined to get every piece of the anatomy exactly correct, he stole into the church mortuary and dissected a dead man for a better understanding of the tendons, muscles, bones, and fat beneath the surface of the skin. David, a humble figure from the biblical story that pitted him against a giant, was commissioned by the Republic of Florence itself and displayed proudly in the main plaza. The statue came to represent Florentine principles of humanism, republicanism, and artistic and literary freedom.

In 1508, another of Michelangelo's greatest commissions was granted—the ceiling of the Sistine Chapel in Vatican City. His painting matched his sculpture for talent and realism, and the four-year period it took to complete the work solidified the artist's reputation as one of the great minds of the Renaissance. Finally, Michelangelo had the praise and fame he had desired since coming to study at Lorenzo de' Medici's academy. At the age of 88, he died in Rome and was buried in Florence.

Chapter 12 – Copernicus

With the advent of complex sciences and mathematics, educated people everywhere wanted to unveil the secrets of the night sky. Though the Catholic Church was often wary of the practice of peering closely into what it considered God's private creations, the phenomenon that was astronomy was simply too exciting to keep from observers like Nicolaus Copernicus. Born in Royal Prussia, a region of the Kingdom of Poland, in 1473, Copernicus spent much of his life making sense of the paths of stars in the sky, introducing the faith-shattering theory that it was not Earth at the center of the universe but the sun.

This went against what all educated people at the time had been taught about the model of the universe created by Ptolemy in the 2nd century CE. Based on Aristotle's assertion that the Earth was a stationary object around which the heavenly bodies that were the moon and stars moved, Ptolemy drew up a model of this system that described perfectly circular paths for the sun and moon with the Earth at the center. Heavily reinvested in classic science and philosophy, Renaissance Europe was not easy to convince that a renowned Greek could possibly be wrong.

Mostly because of mankind's egocentrism and the fact that the Catholic Bible refers to the Earth as the center of all things, astronomic theories up to this point assumed that the sun, moon, planets, and stars traveled around the Earth according to Aristotle's and Ptolemy's descriptions. Many confusing charts and scientific models were constructed to try to explain the patterns each celestial body made in the sky from this standpoint, each with confounding loops intended to account for the backward—or retrograde—motion of some stars. To Copernicus, there seemed to be a different explanation to each pattern: The Earth itself was moving, perhaps even spinning. His solution was eloquent and simple, just what natural scientists then and now strive for.

In 1532, Copernicus finished his first complete draft of *De Revolutionibus Orbium Coelestium*—in English, *On the Revolutions of the Heavenly Spheres*—but he did not put it in print. Instead, already familiar with the Church's dislike of his subject matter, he merely shared the handwritten version with people he trusted. The theory was spoken of in some circles but remained independent until the astronomer was convinced by a pupil to send it to Germany to be printed. It was not published until 1543, the same year Copernicus died at the age of 70. The book was diplomatically dedicated to Pope Paul III. The scientist further entreated his work to the context of Catholicism in hopes of it being taken seriously (as quoted in *Poland: The Knight Among Nations*):

> To know the mighty works of God, to comprehend His wisdom and majesty and power; to appreciate, in degree, the wonderful workings of His laws, surely all this must be a pleasing and acceptable mode of worship to the Most High, to whom ignorance cannot be more grateful than knowledge.

The sycophantic remarks did little good. Even Martin Luther, leader of the new and more humanistic religion, saw only blasphemy in the pages of *Heavenly Spheres*.

As for Nicolaus Copernicus, the remains of one of Poland's—and the world's—greatest scientists were buried in an unmarked grave at Frombork Cathedral, lost until 2005. Genetic scientists helped identify the uncovered bones of their accomplished colleague by matching the DNA from the grave site with hairs left in Copernicus' own books. The polymath's bones were blessed by Poland's clerics and reburied with reverence, marked with a black granite stone adorned with a model of the solar system.

Chapter 13 – The Reformation

While new humanist ideologies were being discussed from Italy to Ireland, religious philosophy began to evolve in small pockets of Europe. Educated free-thinkers who studied religious texts very closely wondered if there weren't perhaps sections of the Catholic Gospels that had been misinterpreted or translated poorly from their original Greek. One such man was Martin Luther, born in the County of Mansfeld within the Holy Roman Empire. Luther's personal belief that salvation from God could be achieved through means other than those professed in the Bible was a revolutionary idea, but it caught on quickly. In 1517, Luther published *Disputation on the Power of Indulgences*, which made him a swift enemy of the Holy Roman Empire and Pope Leo X (born Giovanni di Lorenzo de' Medici). Luther's continued writings enraged the most devout of Catholic Europe.

The First Commandment

You must not have other gods.

That is, I must be your only God.

Question: What does this saying mean? How should we understand it? What does it mean to have a god? What is God?

> Answer: To have a god means this: You expect to receive all good things from it and turn to it in every time of trouble. Yes, to have a god means to trust and to believe in Him with your whole heart. I have often said that only the trust and faith of the heart can make God or an idol. If your faith and trust are true, you have the true God, too. On the other hand, where trust is false, is evil, there you will not have the true God either. Faith and God live together. I tell you, whatever you set your heart on and rely on is really your god.

After writing his argument for better treatment of humankind during their lifetimes—versus waiting for rewards in the afterlife—Luther reportedly nailed his document to the door of a Catholic Church. In addition, his *Indulgences* book attacked a basic premise of the contemporary Church, that is the payment in exchange for the removal of sins. It was a common practice, and of course, since real money was involved, only the wealthy could afford to shorten their time in purgatory. Fifty years later, the selling of indulgences was made illegal by Pope Pius V, but that's not all Luther had to say about the state of the Church. Luther's principal argument against Catholicism was that it required its followers to accept biblical translations and interpretations as given to them by their appointed clerics. Why not, Luther argued, allow the common people to read the words for themselves and find their own truth in the Gospels? It was this premise that captured the humanistic ideologies of the time, inspiring people throughout Europe to look past the doctrine of the bishops and priests and discover religion on their own terms. Luther's ideas were first implemented in the weak holdings of the Holy Roman Empire and its satellite polities.

During much of the Middle Ages, modern Austria was the political entity known as the Duchy of Bavaria, which was subsumed by the Holy Roman Empire. This was also the case for various sections of modern Germany, Italy, and Slovenia. These areas were not centrally led by the Holy Roman Empire but managed by family members of the powerful House of Habsburg. This political organization led to largely independent duchies which may or may not have followed the doctrine of the Holy Roman Empire to the letter. It was in many of these regions that religious reform first began to take hold.

With Charles V, House of Habsburg, named Holy Roman Emperor in 1519, the Protestant-friendly corners of the empire came under close scrutiny. Though the management of the duchies was in the hands of his own family, Charles V knew perfectly well not everyone could be trusted to enforce Christianity. In particular, the problem was not so much that a few outlying Habsburgs believed in the Protestant religion, but that they took a lax attitude with respect to their subject German princes. It simply didn't matter one way or another to Charles' relatives whether their regions practiced Catholicism to the letter so long as their taxes were paid. This made a great deal of the far-reaching Holy Roman Empire fertile for new ideas and new leadership.

Luther was not the only proponent of a non-Catholic system during this period. His peers, John Calvin and Ulrich Zwingli, also preached against the stranglehold of Catholicism, opting to impart their own interpretation of the Gospels upon Christian followers. The details of Lutheranism, Calvinism, and Zwinglism vary and were sometimes points of contention even between Protestants, but all were stimuli for the Reformation as a whole, and each played an important part in the changed religious fabric of the continent.

The first duchy to officially become Lutheran was not a Habsburg holding but that of the Hohenzollern line. Albert Hohenzollern converted to Lutheranism in the early 16th century and established the church in his jurisdiction, the Duchy of Prussia, in 1525. It was the very first Lutheran state in Europe, soon followed by the jurisdictions of Albert's brother George, the Duchies of Silesia and Franconia. Together, the Hohenzollern dukes and their Scandinavian in-laws showed the potential of Lutheranism—then still championed by Martin Luther himself—to the rest of Europe. Under lazy or underfunded Habsburg rule, the Duchies of Wurttemberg and Pomerania soon followed suit.

Converting to Lutheranism gave local dukes and regional landlords the opportunity to throw off the official shackles of the Catholic-decreed political landscape and claim the lands they administrated for themselves. Politically speaking, the regions in question would suffer decades of authoritative tug-of-war, but the new religion remained quite firm. By the end of the 16th century, much of modern Germany and Switzerland were Protestant, as well as Sweden, Denmark, the Netherlands, England, Ireland, and Scotland.

In Spain, France, Portugal, and the remaining Holy Roman Empire, Catholicism—and the Inquisition—still reigned.

Chapter 14 – The Spanish Inquisition and Renaissance

Spain was something of a political mosaic in the Late Middle Ages, comprised of the Kingdoms of Navarre, Castile, Aragon, Leon, Galicia, and multiple Catalan states. Much of the southern half of modern Spain and Portugal were, at the time, inhabited and ruled by Muslims. For centuries, Catholics and Muslims fought for control of the entire region, and eventually, the Catholic monarchs were victorious in the late 15th century. In 1469, the marriage of Queen Isabella of Castile and King Ferdinand II of Aragon marked the beginning of the eventual unification of Spain and the intensification of Catholic fervor throughout the Iberian Peninsula.

After successfully wresting control of the last Islamic holdout—Granada—within Iberia, Isabella and Ferdinand were more determined than ever to create the most devout Christian kingdom in the world. Now that their primary military campaign had ended, they turned their energies toward the development of the Tribunal of the Holy Office of the Inquisition in 1478. They started by ordering all people in Castile to convert immediately to Catholicism or leave the kingdom altogether. At least 40,000 people chose to leave, mostly to

Portugal or North Africa. Once the Jews and Muslims of the realm had converted, spies and secret police in the king and queen's employ searched for signs that the newly-baptized Christians were still practicing their original faiths.

Despite its historical fame, the Spanish Inquisition was not the first of its kind, nor was it the only regional Inquisition in Catholic Europe. The revamped program that was launched by Ferdinand and Isabella was actually a replacement for what they viewed as an inefficient and outdated system of faith surveillance. Begun in the 12th century, the Inquisition had offices in Rome, Florence, Venice, Portugal, and France. In the 15th century, the local offices of the Spanish Inquisition were given renewed resources to hunt and find members of the community who did not fit into the religious template as dictated by the Church.

Second to those of the Jewish faith, Anglicans and Protestants were the most hunted throughout Spain by the 21 tribunals of the Grand Inquisitor. Though there were relatively very few members of these faiths present in Spain to begin with, those routed out by the Inquisition were dealt with harshly. At least 100 Protestants were burned alive under King Philip II, and these executions did not only take place in continental Spain—Mexico, Lima, and other New World holdings were under the same administration as their colonial peers. Over 1,000 supposed heretics were burned throughout Spain and its colonies before the end of the 17th century, including bigamists, homosexuals, witches, Muslims, and other non-Catholics. Muslim converts to Catholicism were also evicted from Spain en masse starting in 1609.

Though philosophical and religious reform was not in the cards for Spain, the kingdom of Isabella and Ferdinand can truly be said to have joined the Renaissance just before the turn of the 16th century. Thanks to the political power the monarchy seized for itself through careful warfare, marriages, and naval expeditions, a great deal of the Spanish realm had enough economic stability to pursue literature and fine arts. Antonio de Nebrija's book, *Gramática de la Lengua*

Castellana, was a linguistic turning point for all of Spain, describing the rules and uses of the kingdom's common language. It was the very first such book of a Western European language besides Latin, and its creation meant that Spanish rulers could not only use its contents to teach conquered nations to speak like a Spaniard but that all existing principalities of the unified country could be expected to communicate in the same language. Castellana (Castilian) became perceived as the most important languages spoken in the kingdom, the one used by the most educated and wealthy of the nation. It worked so well that today the language is simply referred to as Spanish.

Humanism, in perhaps a milder form than in other parts of the continent, did find its way across Spanish borders to take root in the minds of philosophers and scientists of the day, inspiring the creation of the School of Salamanca. Realizing that Catholicism was under attack from great thinkers and writers across Europe, Francisco de Vitoria helped found the school so that he and other Spanish intellectuals could consider their place in the world. Vitoria and his peers followed the teachings of the Italian Thomas Aquinas, a Catholic priest and influential theologian of the day.

Mostly unwilling to consider an existence outside of Catholicism, Aquinas, Vitoria, and Spanish philosophers looked at humanism as it directly related to the rights of humankind itself. They decided that since humans were a natural part of the world, they were all born with the same basic rights and freedoms as one another—at least in theory, if not in practice. Even having attempted to stay within the confines of Catholicism, the Salmanticenses hit upon a philosophy that ran headfirst into dogmatic conflict with the Church. Under Spanish law, no non-Catholics had any rights to own land, marry, or even live in Spain.

However, Isabella and Ferdinand felt the religious cleansing of their kingdoms was the best way forward to unite all of Spain under their crowns. Called "The Catholic Monarchs" by the rest of Europe, their reign is considered the beginning of the Spanish nation. Devout to a fault, the monarchs of Castile and Aragon set up their own Inquisition to replace what they viewed as a defunct and ineffective punishment system for blasphemers and heretics. They declared all citizens of Spain Catholics and with the support of the papacy became the most powerful couple in Europe. Everyone, including enemies like England, wanted to ally with them.

After Ferdinand and Isabella's deaths, their grandson Charles V—a Habsburg—inherited the new Spanish Kingdom, along with the Holy Roman Empire and the Kingdom of Italy. The most powerful monarch in all of Christian Europe, Charles found himself constantly at war in Italy and hounded by the progress of Protestantism in his outlying lands. As was in keeping with Habsburg character, however, Charles V was a patron of Spanish arts, allowing the happy growth of music, literature, and painting during his rule. Pedro Calderon and Lope de Vega wrote scripts for the burgeoning Spanish theater and opera houses, while Tomas Luis de Victoria composed classical vocal music as his soundtrack to the times. Herrerian and Baroque-style palaces graced the cityscapes of Valladolid, Barcelona, and Madrid, while massive domed cathedrals were built in continuing honor of the Catholic faith.

The century beginning in 1492 is called Spain's *Siglo de Oro*, or its Golden Age. It began under the strict rule of Isabella and Ferdinand before passing to Charles V and finally Phillip II, who died in 1598.

Chapter 15 – France and the Wars of Religion

Suffering heavily from the Black Death while Italy and other countries stretched their artistic and philosophical legs, France was a relatively latecomer to the Renaissance. Some historians mark its beginning by the French invasion of Italy in 1494, and though this is a controversial starting point, it is true that French art and culture blossomed most noticeably during the 16th and 17th centuries. It is perhaps somewhat ironic that the term "renaissance" is a French word used by the 19th-century French historian, Jules Michelet, to label the period in which France itself was late to join.

France's great achievements during this period were many, from nationalistic political philosophies and Burgundian style textured music to sculpted gardens and short stories—but perhaps above all these things, it is French Renaissance architecture that stands out. It is within the borders of a nation that once comprised the Duchies of Aquitaine, Brittany, Normandy, Flanders, and Counties of Toulouse, Champagne, and Flanders, among others, that the epitome of fairy tale castles reached their greatest height. At a time when the French kingdom was mostly consolidated, noble residences no longer necessarily needed to be built as fortresses.

Ironically, the citizens of a politically united France were at war with one another over the correct form of Christianity. French Catholics labeled their Protestant brothers and neighbors Huguenots and persecuted them violently in the name of God. Meanwhile, the Crown looked to prettier things, like fancy châteaux and lush landscaping.

During the 16th century, French Renaissance architecture was fairly strictly copied from contemporary Italians. The stylistic theft occurred after French King Charles VIII sent troops into Naples, looking to dislodge the Spanish army and claim the city for himself. Charles was ultimately ousted, but not before he had a chance to admire all the stunning new buildings and landscaped gardens of Naples. The king didn't go home empty-handed, either—he took over twenty Italian craftsmen back with him to France, intent on remodeling his own Château d'Amboise. The project ensued just three years after Charles' gothic remodel of the very same château. Domenico da Cortona and Fra Giocondo were the Italian masonry architects responsible for the new design. Pacello da Mercogliano was given free rein over the gardens so that the château was recreated in all its Italian splendor just in time for the king to die there in 1498.

Amboise became a beacon by which much of the future architecture of Paris was compared. Leonardo da Vinci was invited to the Château in 1516 by King Francis I, and the polymath lived and worked at the Château Clos Luce—connected to Amboise via underground tunnel—for the remaining three years of his life. Both the Italian building style and the Italian master of arts and engineering made a long-lasting impression on the French capital that would help inspire its resident artists and great thinkers.

Fresh ideas moving in from the east from the likes of da Vinci, da Cortona, and Giocondo put French humanists in an awkward position, given that they shared a significant border with the Habsburg Empire. Influenced by Protestantism, anti-Catholic rhetoric, and a wave of secular sciences while simultaneously keeping the peace with a nation of fervent, Inquisitive Catholics, France dared not to lean too far to any one side. Lords and philosophers alike watched in horror as the wave of Lutheranism and Calvinism flooded their way, overwhelming England to the west and enraging the Habsburg Empire to the east. For parliamentarian Jean Bodin (1530-1596), the struggle between tradition and the new religion resembled his inner thoughts on the subject. The Wars of Religion that plagued the Kingdom of France between 1562 and 1598 weighed heavily on the nation, and enlightened minds who may otherwise have chosen a side thought better of it in search of national peace.

A true Renaissance man, Bodin studied Roman law at the University of Toulouse before teaching at his alma mater. He stayed at the school throughout the 1550s and tried to gain support for a department of humanist learning but failed before leaving the university in 1560. Finished with teaching, Bodin worked closely with the royal Valois family and served as a member of the Parlement and a delegate of the Third Estate (the common people). His political role was essentially that of a political speaker and advisor within the Crown's Parlement.

Bodin favored a strong monarchy over the divisive new religions and governments created under Protestantism. Though he agreed with the Lutheran idea that a church should not hold power over the government or its king, he disliked such a force that could shake the foundations of nationalism and threaten the state altogether, as it did when Catholic France attacked the Huguenots. Bodin believed in a strong and unified France, and if anything, he preferred the Crown have more power to put down the violence rather than flounder under the weight of potential religious reforms.

Quite conservative in comparison to his eastern humanist peers, Bodin officially swore an oath to the Catholic Church along with his fellow Parlement members. In retrospect, there was little choice for Bodin or any of his colleagues. Personally, however, it is likely that religion was not at the forefront of his decision-making. When sent to England with Prince Francis in 1581, he opted not to ask the English Queen Elizabeth I to provide her Catholic subjects with better treatment. Edmund Campion, an English Catholic priest, was imprisoned and executed for performing illegal non-Anglican services while Bodin was abroad at Elizabeth's court. After Campion was hung, the French diplomat wrote a public letter calling for a stop to violent punishment in response to religious matters. He had certainly seen enough of such things in his own country.

At home, the religious wars gained momentum under the regency leadership of Queen Catherine de' Medici. After the death of her son, Francis II, in 1560, the Italian queen came into power since her remaining son was only ten years old. France, on the whole, was unhappy under a foreign monarch and particularly concerned about whether Catherine would try to force them to convert to the Catholic religion of her native Florence. Indeed, it seemed the French Crown wanted to achieve peace between the two religious factions within its kingdom when Queen Catherine and her son, King Charles IX, arranged the mixed-faith wedding of French Princess Margaret of Valois to Protestant Henry III of Navarre.

The wedding turned out to be a murderous plot, as when Paris was full of important Huguenots who had attended the wedding on August 18th, 1572, King Charles IX ordered them all to be executed. The massacre began the night before St. Bartholomew's Day and continued on for days afterward, radiating out of the city and into the smaller villages outlying the capital. Even a favorite of the king, Huguenot Admiral de Coligny, was ordered to be struck down mercilessly. The admiral escaped the first assassination attempt but fell during the wider violence of the following days.

Protestant leaders of the time, Coligny included, had come to have great mistrust in Queen Catherine, who wouldn't allow her son to speak privately with his Huguenot friends. She was known to hold most of the power of the Crown despite her son being over twenty years of age, and it is widely believed that Catherine was the mastermind behind both the wedding and the subsequent murderous rampage of Catholic Paris. This seems very likely, particularly because of the blatant attacks specifically on Coligny, whom the king would probably have tried to spare from death. Even a Catholic priest told his followers during the strife that if the king ordered the Protestants to die, then it was their duty to carry out those wishes.

When the violence ended, almost all of France's Protestant leaders were dead or in hiding, and there was no more illusion about the future of the Huguenot cause. Curiously, however, Margaret chose to distance herself from her Catholic roots and followed the cause of her new husband, Henry III of Navarre. She did so delicately and without causing a great family schism, which ironically made the interfaith wedding—disaster though the celebrations were—a peaceful success. Henry III, now known as Henry IV became king of France in 1589, the first of the House of Bourbon.

Margaret was a powerful and authoritative woman, like her mother, but she was not given to scheming and manipulation as Catherine of Medici has been remembered for. Indeed, Margaret seems to have had a gentler and kinder manner that did not undermine her political and religious leadership.

Chapter 16 – Arts and Politics Across Renaissance Europe

In the Middle Ages and Renaissance, the Netherlands had yet to come into political existence. Instead, seventeen provinces, referred to as the Low Countries, remained in a constant state of economic and military oppression by one of its larger neighbors. Allied with Burgundy, then Spain, and eventually England, Holland's artists and architects were funded well enough to lead the continent in using oil-based paints and the stylistic development of painting itself. The Court of Burgundy often lived in Bruges, and trade goods from France and Italy came through the city regularly to attract merchants, nobles, and artists alike.

While the artists of the Low Countries led the continent with oil painting, Holland's musicians were also making important discoveries. Using flutes, recorders, lyres, lutes, and various brass instruments, Renaissance musicians began to place more importance on the use of their instruments than their predecessors. During the medieval musical period, the focus of the performers, writers, and audience was on human voices working in harmony. Now, the strings, bass, and woodwinds came into sharper focus. They would come to define Renaissance music for all of Europe.

As it transformed literature, so too did the printing press transform music. Musicians needn't hand copy every composition, nor struggle to work with other composers and performers who were musically illiterate. It quickly became easier to teach, learn, and share songs, as well as keep records of the works of each individual composer. Even when a group of musicians had trouble speaking a common language, they could recognize notes and timings on paper. More singers, musicians, and composers were hired by the Church than ever before thanks to economic stability, which gave rise to the practice of wealthy estates hiring on seasonal musical performers.

Though it was not specifically defined by its arts, the most politically powerful nation in Europe throughout the bulk of the Renaissance era was the Holy Roman Empire. Self-important due to its physical ties to ancient Rome and led by an emperor crowned by the Pope himself, it was through alliances with the Empire that smaller kingdoms and principalities of Europe gained wealth and influence. However, as the Protestant faith spread through much of the empire's lands and neighboring states, Emperor Charles V faced continued pressure from France and the Duchies to make reforms. Under his leadership, the empire's authority began to seriously wane, and the empire found itself mostly at war with itself and in defense of the Catholic faith.

In the words of Florentine diplomat, humanist, writer, and historian Niccolò Machiavelli, (1469 – 1527), "Anyone who determines to act in all circumstances the part of a good man must come to ruin among so many who are not good. Hence, if a prince wishes to maintain himself, he must learn how not to be good, and to use that ability or not as is required." The quotation comes from Machiavelli's book, *The Prince*, published in 1532, and it is largely because of this book that the term "Machiavellian" was termed to refer to a shrewd and manipulative political figure. His theories were not pretty, but they stood the test of time, underscoring the methods used by Florentine leaders and emperors of the Holy Roman Empire.

In the late 15th century, when the Medici family had fallen out of its position of authority in Florence, the Machiavelli family seized power for itself. It was a politically frightening time in which Catholic popes and the Holy Roman Empire sought to consolidate power with the remaining Italian states of Sicily and Venice. Constant in-fighting and international marriages between monarchs and their family members defined the time; meanwhile, Niccolo Machiavelli pondered the best methods by which to retain control and profit from his position.

Niccolo Machiavelli was a unique figure in that his political theories were unidealized—that is, he explained historical and contemporary power grabs as he saw them, and simply mimicked the successful strategies of others. His written works on leadership did not strive to portray leadership as some reverent, humble state in which a man works to benefit his subjects but rather as a position of manipulation and conquest. His lack of empathy for the lower classes and people outside of his family characterized him as a somewhat evil figure. In truth, he was a realist and a republican who was just as influenced by humanism as many of his peers.

Though it seemed to be in political turmoil, Florence was still a leader in Renaissance arts during Machiavelli's time. In the 16th and 17th centuries, all of Europe's capital cities were flourishing, full of music, sculpture, paintings, and their own political philosophies. Secularism in politics emerged, humanism allowed people to discern inequitable class divides, and artists had a big, brand new subject to imagine on the other side of the Atlantic Ocean.

It would be a very long time before professional artists had the opportunity to visit, sketch, paint, and interact with lands outside of Europe, but that didn't stop them from visualizing them. Possibly the first European depiction of the Americas was painted by Pinturicchio, only to be forgotten under centuries of grime in its place at the Vatican. Recently restored by professionals, the picture, which ostensibly portrays the resurrection of Jesus, was discovered to feature tiny naked people in the background, adorned in feather headdresses.

It was just the sort of scene that the Spanish pope, Alexander VI, would have heard described to him from messengers from the New World. What were the figures doing in a depiction of an important biblical event? Perhaps Pinturicchio was simply too excited at the idea of an exotic new culture to keep his paintbrush from coloring them into life. His thrill at the notion was shared by rich and poor alike, and just as it immediately touched the art world, so too did the exploration of seas and lands far from Europe touch politics, religion, and the economy for centuries to come.

Chapter 17 – The Age of Discovery

The 15th century ushered in a three-hundred-year period of exploration which saw European nations colonize vast regions of the outside world. The Prince of Portugal, AKA Henry the Navigator, sailed down the western and northern coasts of Africa in search of new routes to India and China, as well as new territories to explore. The Spanish Crown sent its own explorers, as did France and England, all in a bid to become the biggest, most powerful empire since the Romans. Their first goal, however, was trade.

Spices, precious metals, cotton, wheat, and slaves were the most lucrative goods on the European market at the time, and it was the hope of every ship's captain to find enough of these resources to fund forthcoming expeditions and send money home to their families. In Africa, Prince Henry of Portugal started settlements in the Azores and Madeira and stretched his country's influence across the northern coast of Africa, establishing trading ports where Asian and Muslim merchants came to trade. Portuguese merchants sold guns and bought spices, gold, ivory, and pepper. A few merchants specialized in trading guns for slaves, the latter of which were captured by their own countrymen.

Portugal was a kingdom that was already built upon slaves, and therefore its merchant class thought very little of trading gold for human lives. In fact, in 1455, Pope Nicolas V granted Portugal explicit rights to continue the West African slave trade so long as merchants promised to convert the captured people into Catholics. With Prince Henry in charge of every African voyage, he organized the trips so that captives were baptized before they were brought to Lisbon for sale. When criticized for their cruel methods of capture and shipment, the slave traders claimed it was all justified by the Catholic baptism.

Prince Henry died in 1460, having brought his kingdom to the forefront of European colonial efforts and established the precedent for continued African slave trading. By 1490, an estimated 2,000 black slaves arrived in Lisbon every year. As a product, West African slaves proved more popular than the North African, mostly Moroccan, slaves who had been captured before the Portuguese discovered much of the Western African coast. Though there were a handful of black people in Europe before Portugal's merchants entered the picture, these perfectly free and independent travelers were overwhelmed by the influx of thousands of slaves who were put to work in fields and domestic situations. It was at this point that the racial divide began to be set into place, dark skin denoting a classless label of servitude that would not begin to be healed for several centuries.

Portugal's imperial expansion afterward focused mostly on Guinea and the outlying islands of Western Africa. In the early 16th century, Portuguese sailors discovered the vast Pacific Ocean. The next great cartological development, from a European perspective, happened in 1492 at the expense of the next great naval nation: Spain. One of the most significant events of the Renaissance took place when an Italian explorer named Cristoforo Colombo, more commonly known today as Christopher Columbus, sailed west and discovered land beyond any that had previously been mapped by Europeans. Colombo's discovery had several meaningful outcomes: More Europeans would immediately visit the so-called New World to draw maps and seek out saleable goods, and they would try to stake claim over it. The most significant monarchy in the early exploration and colonization of the Americas was that of Spain since it was under the patronage of Queen Isabella of Castile that the voyage had been conducted.

Isabella originally agreed to help fund Colombo's expedition on the expectation that he would find a quicker route to India and therefore increase Spain's potential earnings in the spice trade. When that plan failed, she quickly saw the promise of much more than a short journey to India: she saw a whole new continent to lead to the Catholic Church. Dubbed "Isabella the Catholic" by the pope himself, the Queen of Castile believed she was called by God to save the souls of the people across the Atlantic Ocean. Colombo and subsequent Spanish explorers could easily gain her favor by promising to preach Catholicism once they reached the shores of the New World, thereby hoping to convert the natives.

Colombo and successive Spanish conquistadors made the promises they needed to make in order to find funding for their journeys and then largely followed their own rules once out of Europe. The first official European settlement in the Americas was the small colony of La Navidad, founded by Colombo in the name of Spain. He left 39 settlers there in December of 1492 in what is modern Haiti. Hailed by European-descended Americans as the man responsible for changing the future of the New World and the Old World simultaneously, Colombo truly was a man of his own will, beholden to no one. He participated in the genocide of non-hostile native communities of people, facilitated the trade of native slaves—including very young girls for sexual purposes—and required friendly native people to pay him tribute in the form of gold. Furthermore, Colombo was in fact not the first European explorer to discover part of the Americas, as Viking crews had already landed and settled in modern Newfoundland nearly 500 years earlier.

Not to be left behind on the other side of the Atlantic, Portugal moved in soon enough to claim the large piece of South America that is now Brazil. Spain fought its own way across the central and southern lands of the Americas, exterminating native people, destroying ancient cities and structures, and rebranding them under Spanish flags. In this way, Spain founded Mexico, France took control of many Caribbean islands, and England and France gained control in much of North America.

Ironically, the bulk of American landmass discoveries—on the part of English sailor Henry Hudson, Portuguese explorer Ferdinand Magellan, and their counterparts—were the result of expensive attempts to reach Asia by sailing west. Astronomers and sailors were confident by that point that the Earth was a globe, but the idea of sailing in the opposite direction to one's final destination was still uncomfortable for most. It took courage to sail westward across the Atlantic in search of India or China, but once Colombo landed at San Salvador Island, others were motivated to attempt the same voyage.

John Cabot reached Newfoundland in the name of England in 1497; Portuguese explorer João Fernandes Lavrador reached and mapped Newfoundland and Labrador in 1499; Pedro Álvares Cabral found Brazil in 1500, again for Portugal; and Colombo himself found Venezuela and Panama, plus other southern locations in his next voyages.

It was indeed an Age of Discovery, a time when the most powerful European kingdoms spread their wings, navigators and builders developed stronger sailing vessels, and people became aware of their place in the rest of the world. Those who had the money and influence to do so took what they wanted and planted flags to justify their actions. For many generations of educated Renaissance Europeans, the physical world seemed to be opening up alongside the philosophical, religious, and scientific discoveries at home. For the inhabitants of those "newly discovered" parts of the world, it was a period of disease, political uncertainty, subjugation, and war that ultimately led to an immense boom in the African slave trade.

Once more, thousands of black hostages were baptized and shipped away from home, only to find themselves in hostile land under the violent authority of whoever paid the most money. African and indigenous slaves were forced to do the bidding of their heavily-armed European masters, further cementing the perceived divide in social hierarchy in relation to pale or dark skin. Even as Spain, England, Portugal, France, and other colonial powers slowly built their overseas empires, the status and relative quality of life for dark-skinned people did not improve.

Chapter 18 – Women's Education

Even before the oppression and exploitation of Africans and Native Americans, there was one facet of Dark Age Europe that was repeatedly excluded from higher learning, regardless of age or wealth: women. From the poorest peasants to the noblest princesses, females were taught the lessons most pertinent to managing their households and kept out of extensive literacy, philosophy, science, and rhetoric lessons. Poor women learned from their mothers how to prepare food, repair clothing, and maintain gardens and livestock, while daughters of landowners, royals, and wealthy families were taught a watered-down version of such skills. When the Renaissance took hold of Europe, the importance placed on higher education finally started to include more girls and women.

> Not all men (and especially the wisest) share the opinion that it is bad for women to be educated. But it is very true that many foolish men have claimed this because it displeased them that women knew more than they did.

So wrote Christine de Pizan in her 15th-century novel, *The Book of the City of Ladies*. It was an astonishing book that not only used its content to speak up for women, but that broke with tradition simply by having been written by a woman. Active as a writer in both Italy and France, de Pizan was born in Venice to a polymath father who served as a doctor, councilor, and court astrologer. Christine de Pizan was one of the few females in the High Middle Ages to enjoy a full education, let alone to pick up a quill and put stories on parchment.

Finding herself a widow without legal recourse to her dead husband's estate, de Pizan cared for her children by selling stories. She was popular enough to come to the attention of many members of the Venetian, Italian, and French courts, and the latter supported her as patrons. Much in the same vein as court painters, musicians, and entertainers, emerging storytellers like de Pizan found a place for themselves among the wealthy. De Pizan was an early example of a phenomenon that grew more important over the successive centuries of the Renaissance: female professionalism.

Women of both the upper and lower classes in Europe were hugely underrepresented in literature, politics, and even the physical household of the Middle Ages. Females of noble families were kept under strict surveillance and taught how to conduct themselves quietly and respectfully while maintaining their husband's home and tending to their children and servants. Though this overwhelmingly continued to be the norm during the Renaissance, there was a great deal more women allowed to pursue higher education and creative occupations than ever before. Several examples include none other than the royals of Europe themselves: Catherine de' Medici, Queen of France; Mary Stuart, Queen of Scotland; and Mary and Elizabeth Tudor, as well as most of the wives of King Henry VIII.

Of course, the education of females put the age-old question to the test—did girls have the same intellectual capacity as boys? Then—as now, unfortunately—male decision-makers had trouble believing their oppressed sisters, wives, and mothers could handle the pressures of mathematics, science, literature, and governance. De Pizan pushed back against the onslaught of patriarchy in her writing, specifically addressing her belief that women's minds would flourish under excellent tutorship.

> If it were customary to send little girls to school and teach them the same subjects as are taught to boys, they would learn just as fully and would understand the subtleties of all arts and sciences.

For royal women, the opportunity to become highly educated became almost as mandatory as it was for royal males. Both sons and daughters of mighty monarchs learned from their tutors as well as their parents the various methods of governance and diplomacy so that kings could come to rely on their queens to rule during prolonged absences. Thus was the case with England's King Henry VIII and his first wife, Queen Catherine of Aragon.

Henry and Catherine were matched by their royal parents to bring an end to constant political strife between their two kingdoms. Catherine, daughter of the infamous Isabella and Ferdinand, grew up in the brave, capable shadow of her commanding mother. Probably as a direct result of such parentage and example, Queen Catherine took the regency of England quite seriously when her kingly husband was away fighting over French lands during 1513. With Henry VIII away, England's constant enemy, the Scots, took the chance to invade their southern neighbor. Between the quick administrations of Catherine and her husband's advisor, Lord Surrey, the enemy army was crushed and the King of Scotland himself killed in battle. Catherine arranged for the bloodied coat of Scotland's King James IV to be sent to her husband in France.

Queen Catherine's education and her early exposure to military strategy via her mother and father proved satisfactory in preparing her to succeed in a man's role. Proud of her achievements on the throne, Catherine made absolutely certain that her only child and daughter, Mary, received as full an education as she had. To facilitate this goal, the queen commissioned a book from Spanish humanist writer Juan Luis Vives entitled *The Education of a Christian Woman*.

Vives' book, subtitled *A 16th-century Manual*, covered various personal topics as they related to young, unmarried women, married women, and twice-married or widowed women. These lessons mostly explained how Catherine's ideal Christian lady should behave toward herself, her suitors, and her husband. Though the sciences were under intense development within England and its neighboring kingdoms, neither Tudor women nor average men were particularly pressed to pursue a scientific career. Rather, both were encouraged to develop their knowledge of religion and personally develop upon existing religious philosophy for the whole span of their lives. Henry VIII, his wives, and children were avid religious philosophers, particularly on the subject of the Church of England and Protestantism (with the exception of Mary, a staunch Catholic like her mother Catherine).

Queen Catherine didn't only see to the education of her daughter but also became a trusted patron of Queens' College of Cambridge, an educational facility whose establishment and support was passed through the hands of many Renaissance queens of England, from Margaret of Anjou in 1448 to Elizabeth Woodville in 1465, then to Margaret Beaufort, mother of King Henry Tudor VII after the Wars of the Roses were concluded in 1485. Though her husband was not a regular donor to England's universities, Queen Catherine ensured that Queens' College was debt-free and even put money into the establishment of St. John's College, which had been a dear wish of the late Margaret Beaufort.

Unfortunately, even with royal female patronage, women were by and large not allowed to earn a university degree until the 20th century. In earlier centuries they could perhaps attend lectures or follow along with classes if they had the permission of their fathers or male relatives; however, universities remained the domain of the male. It has even been questioned whether or not the female sex actually experienced the European Renaissance at all.

Chapter 19 – Galileo Galilei

Once more in the Duchy of Florence, a polymath appeared in 1564 by the name of Galileo Galilei. Encouraged by his father to attend the University of Pisa and join the medical field, instead, young Galileo found himself transfixed on the study of physical objects and their movements. He switched his studies to mathematics and natural sciences and as a result became one of the most important astronomers and physicists of his time. Perhaps his longest-lasting contribution to science was the further development of an existing piece of technology—the telescope—into astronomy's most important tool.

Lenses were already changing how nearsighted and farsighted people saw the world, but when an unknown innovator realized that two lenses together could produce an exponential magnifying effect, the telescope was born. Galileo took this knowledge and crafted his own glass lenses, teaching himself how to curve and align the lenses ideally so that the magnification effect was at its greatest. Galileo's 8x magnifying scope was purchased by the military, whom he had convinced could use it to see their enemies before being spotted themselves. For himself, however, the new design had a more exciting purpose: revealing the night sky. It was a scientific revelation that immediately changed how Galileo and his students imagined the universe around their own planet.

A proponent of Copernicus' heliocentric model of the universe, Galileo used his modified telescope to explore the celestial bodies of our own Milky Way Galaxy. First, he turned his telescope to the moon and was shocked to discover that instead of a smooth, flawless surface, the little round ball in the sky was covered in pockmarks and ridges. This discovery didn't mesh well with the biblical assumption that all heavenly bodies were perfect structures.

Still with greater surprise did he note the tiny stars surrounding Jupiter. After watching the movements of these little stars for several weeks, the astronomer realized they were neither stars nor planets but orbiting moons. These were Io, Europa, Ganymede, and Callista. The knowledge of such things was too much to keep to himself, so Galileo published *Sidereous Nuncius*—or *Starry Messenger*—in 1610 to share his findings with the world. It was an instant sensation, invoking simultaneous praise and calls of blasphemy.

In his book, Galileo didn't just explain the movements of Jupiter's moons or describe the marks on our own moon. He sketched out the regularly changing shape of Venus, whose shadow metamorphized the planet from a small disc into a large crescent shape—a movement of sunlight and shadow that belied the planet's solar orbit. It was proof of the Copernican model of the universe.

Galileo's telescopic observations of the sky didn't stop, though he knew perfectly well he was under the critical, dangerous eye of the Inquisition. Using his own lenses, he observed the planet Saturn and kept careful sketches of its unusual appearance in his notes. First believing that the blurry objects on either side of Saturn were moons, Galileo was ultimately at a loss as to what the fixed arches could truly be. He referred to them as ears and was further perplexed when the ears disappeared from view in 1612 only to return in 1613. Not until 1655 would it be suggested that Saturn was actually surrounded by a fixed ring, by the Dutch astronomer Christiaan Huygens. Modern scientists explain the disappearance of the planet's rings in 1612 by telling us Earth had moved into the same plane as the ring, rendering it too thin to be seen by Galileo's relatively weak telescope.

Astronomy was not Galileo's only occupation outside of teaching mathematics. He was interested in physics and contrived various theories of motion and gravity that predate those of Newton. He also wrote extensively on the subject of ocean tides, a phenomenon he believed proved that the Earth was in motion around the sun. His theory was incorrect since it posited that the water acted like a pendulum around the Earth's core, but his observations provided detailed data for further study.

Of course, scientific theories and proofs, such as those Galileo achieved with the use of his telescope, were not without great criticism from the Church. Some critics were merely curious such as the Grand Duchess Christina of Tuscany. Answering her questions as to how his work fit with biblical knowledge, Galileo wrote to her to try to explain himself.

> Some years ago, as Your Serene Highness well knows, I discovered in the heavens many things that had not been seen before our own age. The novelty of these things, as well as some consequences which followed from them in contradiction to the physical notions commonly held among academic philosophers, stirred up against me no small number of professors — as if I had placed these things in the sky with my own hands in order to upset nature and overturn the sciences. They seemed to forget that the increase of known truths stimulates the investigation, establishment, and growth of the arts; not their diminution or destruction.

In time, the scientist was investigated by the Roman Inquisition. The trial took place in 1616 during which Pope Paul V formally asked Galileo to recant his assertion that the universe was centered around the sun. For his own wellbeing, the astronomer did so and was discharged safely from the court and custody of the Inquisition.

Afterward, Galileo took greater care with works that he published, but when Pope Urban VIII came to power in 1623, he was elated due to the fact that the two of them were on friendly terms, as Urban previously championed some of Galileo's earlier work. He committed to writing a book that was expressly commissioned by the new Catholic leader and in his excitement forgot to explicitly follow the pope's instructions. Urban VIII asked Galileo to discuss points both for and against a heliocentric universe then explain which theory he personally found more compelling. Instead, Galileo stated only points supporting the heliocentric theory.

The book, called *Dialogue Concerning the Two Chief World Systems*, was published in 1632, and it was not to the pope's liking. It may not have helped that the fictional character on the side of geocentrism—who Galileo claimed was based on Greek author Simplicius—seemed to speak like the pope. "Simplicio" was then, as now, easily construed as "simpleton."

That same year, Galileo was called back to Rome to speak with the Inquisition. Threatened with torture, he maintained that he had not intended to promote heliocentrism in his book and that he was only doing what had been requested of him by the pope. He was not found guilty but was declared very suspicious of heresy and therefore sentenced to be imprisoned. The sentence was carried out the next day, though Galileo was allowed to remain under house arrest instead of being taken away to a public prison. He remained sequestered at his home for the remainder of his life.

Chapter 20 – English Renaissance Under the Tudors

As the farthest kingdoms west of Italy at the start of the Renaissance, England, Ireland, and Scotland developed along a slightly delayed timeline in terms of higher education and religious reformation. Suffering under an oppressive and resource-depleting civil war for much of the 15th century, England and Ireland lacked stable leadership until 1485, when Henry Tudor defeated King Richard III in battle and took the throne for himself and his direct descendants.

Under 118 years of Tudor rule, England and Ireland found relative peace and prosperity as did their close neighbor, Scotland. King Henry VII, first of his line, cleverly consolidated his power by marrying into his rival family and producing male heirs with full royal blood in their veins. He sent loyal nobles to the far corners of the kingdom to take care of local courts and justice, and established stronger infrastructure in terms of roads and central taxation. By the time Henry's son inherited the kingdom, it had become richer and more powerful than ever before. Truly, the English Renaissance began and ended with the reign of the Tudor Dynasty.

King Henry VIII, who ascended to the throne just prior to his 18th birthday in 1509, took his father's legacy and endeavored to put his own mark on the kingdom. A prideful and nationalistic king, Henry VIII veered away from the diplomacy at which his father excelled and organized various, continued military campaigns abroad. He wanted to claim France in the name of the English throne, driven by the belief that it was his ancestral right. He also wanted to father many strong sons, a feat in which he faltered.

In the 1530s when he met an exciting and attractive young woman named Anne Boleyn, Henry envisaged a way in which he could finally have the large family he craved as well as bring fresh fashion and culture to court. Anne was a lady-in-waiting to Henry's own wife, Catherine of Aragon, but her family and nature were at odds with the reigning queen. Where Anne was a playful, youthful patron of the French arts, Catherine was a steadfast, faithful, and more introverted partner to Henry. Catherine was well-loved by her people, but the couple's lack of sons frustrated the king to the point of divorce.

England, like the rest of Western Europe, was traditionally Roman Catholic and therefore unable to provide divorces for marriages that had been properly performed and consummated. As far as King Henry VIII was concerned, however, he was in charge of his own personal affairs. When the Catholic pope refused to grant Henry the right to divorce Catherine of Aragon so that he could marry Anne Boleyn and have more legitimate children, the king abandoned his lifelong Catholic faith and turned to the new religion that was sweeping Europe: Protestantism.

Under the Protestant doctrine, King Henry VIII knew that he could divorce his wife, emerge from under the proverbial thumb of the Catholic Church, and become the unquestioned leader of his kingdom. It was the ideal solution to every problem he faced, and with visions of legitimate princes and supreme power over the English Church motivating him onward, Henry joined the European Reformation in 1533. It was an epic moment for England and the future Great Britain.

The forthcoming years were tumultuous, to say the least. Still, no sons were born to the king, and Henry shuffled wives constantly in an effort to produce more children and please his extravagant taste for women. Personal issues aside, Henry's Church of England pushed his kingdom headlong into the philosophical and religious discussions occurring throughout the rest of the continent. Finally, England was a contender, worthy of the discourse of neighboring nations who had long debated the benefits and drawbacks of Lutheranism, the possibility that the unquestioned authority of the Catholic Church was self-serving, and the proponents of humanism that related to such religious reforms.

The king's decision had been heartily assisted by the advice of Thomas Cranmer, a Doctor of Divinity at Jesus College. It was the fervent belief of Cranmer that the English king's actions should be judged by an esteemed panel of theologians before his case could be properly dealt with by the pope. Though the pope would never be swayed, Cranmer stayed on as an advisor to King Henry and had a huge impact on how the new church was to be organized, holding the title Archbishop of Canterbury from 1532-1534.

The first step to de-Catholicizing England was the dissolution of the monasteries. Over the course of about four years, Henry VIII saw to it that every Catholic institution within his realm was disbanded. The residents were removed, priests stripped of their power, incomes from the churches, priories, and other Catholic bodies was appropriated by the throne, and all items of value were sold. It was a convenient way for Henry to pay for his ongoing attempts to win power in France. It soon became apparent, however, that the king—himself raised as a devout Catholic—was unwilling to undertake the full transition of England from a Catholic nation into a Protestant kingdom.

When Henry died in 1547, however, the Church of England became the domain of his nine-year-old son Edward VI and his stipulated Regency Council. Edward had been born and raised in the Church of England thanks to his father's reforms, and he was a true believer in the good of pure Protestantism. Even as a young king, Edward transformed England's church with spiritual fervor. Edward put a stop to Mass ceremonies, made it legal for clerics to marry, and declared that England's priests would perform church services in English. At the side of his father's most enthusiastic Protestant reformer, Thomas Cranmer, the young king brought the *Book of Common Prayer* to his people, ending the tradition in which only priests may read from a holy book. Cranmer wrote down his own *39 Articles of Religion* to exactly define just what the Church of England stood for and expected from its constituents, and this was added to the prayer book.

One of the most revolutionary reforms of the Church of England under Edward VI, and later his sister, Elizabeth I, was that common people could now read and discuss the Bible for themselves. Catholicism ruled that commoners were incapable of properly interpreting the Bible's laws on their own and that they must take the word of their priests, bishops, and religious leaders without question. In Reformation England, religious philosophy could truly be explored without fear of the wrath of the Catholic Church. England became a haven for Europeans who were prosecuted by the Spanish Inquisition and the Holy Roman Empire.

Under Queen Mary I, who ruled for 5 years after the death of her 15-year-old brother Edward, England underwent a swift return to Catholicism. Mary's government harshly persecuted Protestants and burned them as heretics. All but Catholics fled the country or hid in the countryside until 1558 when Elizabeth Tudor took the crown. She reigned as a true Protestant queen for 44 years, largely restoring England's reputation in the rest of Europe as a haven of reform, change, and development. The political, religious, and economic stability Elizabeth offered her subjects finally allowed the kingdom to achieve its full Renaissance potential.

Chapter 21 – Shakespeare, Lully, and the New Art

England's so-called Golden Age, the peak of its own Renaissance, came during the reign of Queen Elizabeth I. The last Tudor monarch to hold the throne, Elizabeth I ruled over a prosperous nation whose middle class was educated, trained in a variety of trades, and was largely creative. It was during her reign, between 1558 and 1603, that the very first English theater was built, and the profession of acting and screenwriting took hold of the nation. One of English history's most revered playwrights, William Shakespeare, performed for the queen multiple times.

Shakespeare was by no means the first English playwright, but he was one of the most prolific and has come to exemplify the English Renaissance era. William Shakespeare relocated from Stratford-upon-Avon to London sometime in the 1580s or 1590s, finding work first as an actor and eventually as a scriptwriter. What made his profession so modern was the form his art took—scriptwriting had been a very rare form of writing just a few decades beforehand.

In the Dark Ages of England and continental Europe, theater wasn't altogether unheard of. Short, didactic plays with moral and religious purposes were performed, often as part of a traveling entertainment troupe's show or a church skit used to teach biblical law. Unfortunately, due to the fact that most performers, scriptwriters, and audience members were illiterate during that period of history, very few scripts have survived.

So, what changed during Elizabeth's reign that suddenly made a rare performance art boom in popularity at home and abroad? There were two important changes in England between the Dark Ages and the Renaissance: the threat of death or torture from the Crown for expressive literature and performance was no longer in place, and the improved quality of life in 16th-century Elizabethan England made it possible for more people to spend excess coins on entertainment. No longer was it absolutely necessary to watch every word of a script so that it didn't have an ounce of moral ambiguity, and the industry could flourish under the patronage of the queen herself and a vast audience of wealthy and middle-class people alike.

As Shakespeare discovered his love of writing and theater, he found within it a love of philosophizing about life itself. Like his peers in the Italian and German states, France, and other Renaissance countries, William Shakespeare used his literacy and knowledge of history—gifts due to Tudor education standards—to think about all the modern implications of religion, politics, kingship, and love on the human heart and brain. Perhaps the reason Shakespeare's plays were and are so well-loved is that they explored human nature so well. Unlike the theater shows from centuries before, Shakespeare's works didn't conform to a form in which the audience was expected to learn a lesson. They simply told a story for the sake of an emotional connection between the story and the audience.

In his famous play *Hamlet*, Shakespeare's title character ponders how the knowledge of death and the simple idea of intangible punishments in the afterlife affect the will and behavior of an otherwise bold and daring person.

> But that the dread of something after death,—
>
> The undiscover'd country, from whose bourn
>
> No traveller returns,—puzzles the will,
>
> And makes us rather bear those ills we have
>
> Than fly to others that we know naught of?
>
> Thus conscience does make cowards of us all;
>
> And thus the native hue of resolution
>
> Is sicklied o'er with the pale cast of thought;
>
> And enterprises of great pith and moment,
>
> With this regard, their currents turn awry,
>
> And lose the name of action.

Personal ideologies and philosophies such as these could have brought serious consequences in the era of strict Catholicism, but under Elizabeth, there was legal space for the individual philosopher. It was not only an incredibly modern idea for playwrights and actors, but for audiences as well. Almost every aspect of European life at that point in history was in some way instructed by the church—be it Catholic or otherwise—and the freedom to sit or stand and simply watch a story unfold without taking it too seriously was a huge development in the life of the individual.

While Shakespeare's work focused mostly on romance, comedy, and historical retellings, French theater followed upon its early medieval custom of showing mystery and morality plays to audiences. Although French scriptwriters had been able to grow their industry a century before England, they were tightly controlled in what they wrote and performed due to the close surveillance of the Catholic Church. Morality plays based on the teachings of the Church, therefore, were the simplest to pull off successfully, while more forward-thinking humanist scripts could endanger the entire company of a theater.

Furthermore, French guilds controlled the content of plays and where any such type of play—mystery, tragedy, satire, and farce being the most popular—could be performed. While comedies ruled at court, the common people of France preferred to spend their francs on tragic plays. By the early 17th century, the guilds gave up control of the cities and multiple theater companies moved in, and in the second half of that century, French composers and writers had begun to work together to create an entirely different sort of theater—that of the musical tragedy, or opera. Like so many other cultural aspects of the Renaissance, opera came from Florence.

Dafne was the first show of its type performed in Florence in 1597. It was written by Jacopo Peri in the Baroque musical style that so epitomizes much of European Renaissance musical composition. Though nothing remains of this particular script or its musical composition, the records remain from a performance of *Euridice*, written by Jacopo Peri and Giulio Caccini, presented at the wedding of Henry IV of France and Marie de' Medici. The jump from Florence to Paris was, therefore, entirely precedented: when the new queen of France took up residence with King Henry in Paris, the innovative concept of opera went with her and her retinue. Small versions of the Italian shows were staged haphazardly over the next decades until, in the latter half of the 17th century, French opera truly found its footing.

Throughout the 1670s and 1680s, musician Jean-Baptiste Lully worked extensively with writer Philippe Quinault to produce a catalog of French operas that featured popular actors of spoken stage plays. Like the early Florentine operas, Lully and Quinault's creations usually required actors to sing out full sentences in a regular conversational way rather than conform their words to complex music and master the sort of voicework modern audiences would recognize as operatic.

To show their work to the public, Lully used a tennis court in Bel Air to use as an open-air theater. Soon the operas caught on, and the duo moved from the tennis court to the royal court. Their work unequivocally formed the basis of modern French and European opera and ballet, just as William Shakespeare's work paved the way for modern English stage plays, satire, and comedy. These are the types of cultural changes that typify the European Renaissance on the whole and still stand to represent the blossoming of artistic industries throughout the continent. Indeed, English theater, French ballet, and Italian opera served to unify each respective population during a time of political evolution, giving both artists and patrons something about which to feel proudly patriotic. Much of that feeling still exists today.

Chapter 22 – Seers and Prophets

Science never walked so closely with pseudo-science than it did during the Middle Ages in Europe. Educated people—mostly men—searched earnestly for meaning in the patterns they found around them, interpreting every solar eclipse, meteor shower, and arrangement of twigs in a precise way. Sometimes the Church supported these methods of understanding nature; other times it was quick to label would-be scientists as heretics. Since astronomy had become a fashionable and exciting pursuit, curious researchers looked most often to the stars for guidance.

During this important period of scientific exploration, astronomy was not yet separate from astrology. Therefore, masters of mathematics and medicine who studied the stars and derived prophetic meanings from them were still classed in the highest order with astronomers like Galileo and Copernicus. The telescope was to the Renaissance much what the psychic medium was to Victorian England. The most powerful driving force behind the cult science of astrology was the belief of Plato, Aristotle, and other classic philosophers that the stars could be used to divine the future.

The zodiac, part of ancient astrological practices of the Babylonians and perhaps even the Egyptians, had a part to play in Renaissance stargazing and fortune-telling. As with anything remotely related to the ancient Greeks and Romans, European philosophers jumped on the idea of interpreting the actions of the planets with gusto. They were proud of their efforts, not only because they felt they were restoring their own culture, but because Islamic nations had been continuously making mathematical and scientific discoveries for many centuries by that time.

Motivated by every little reference to the heavens during university lessons, polymaths as early as the 13th century made exciting observations of the sky. One of the first European masters of astronomy was the Italian mathematician, Guido Bonatti. Bonatti's most influential book, *Liber Astronomiae*, or Book of Astronomy, was written around 1277. He used midpoints, a very precise measurement of the location of certain astral bodies within his star chart, to make predictions. He used such calculations to predict that the Count of Montefeltro would succeed in his military campaign but be wounded in doing so. It proved true, making the count a lifelong believer in astrology, and Bonatti's book became an important part of astronomical education for at least two centuries. His calculations were the inspiration for the most prominent astrologers of the Renaissance.

By the 16th century, two such famous astrologers and fortune-tellers were able to use their presumed scientific and spiritual knowledge to serve none other than two powerful European queens: Elizabeth Tudor of England and Catherine de' Medici of France. Nostradamus served the French queen, while John Dee served the English. Both men faced criticism for their professions but simultaneously cultivated the immense trust of their employers.

Dee's start with the royal family was tenuous, in that he was arrested just a few years before Elizabeth took the English throne for having cast her and her sister Mary's horoscopes. Mary was the reigning queen at the time, and it was illegal to cast horoscopes on any member of the royal family—as unsure as the Catholic Church was about how precise any methods of astrology truly were, they were horrified at the idea that one could foretell the death of a monarch. The very suggestion that such futures could be revealed questioned the fabric upon which monarchies and inheritances were based.

Dee found himself in serious trouble when his horoscope calculations landed him with the charge of treason, but he was freed and kept under close scrutiny by church officials. All the same, when Elizbeth replaced her deceased sister in 1558, she sought out the very same man who was criticized of endangering her life with prophecy. Though at that time Dee's most marketable skill was that of navigation, Elizabeth was very much drawn to his knowledge of the occult. She first consulted with him to set the date of her coronation.

Dutifully, John Dee checked his star charts and looked for the best date, one that forecasted luck and fortune. He chose January 15, 1559. Elizabeth happily followed his advice and afterward consulted the man any time she felt anxious about an upcoming date or event. Dee is rumored to have cast a spell on the Spanish Armada, who didn't once successfully breach England's coastline.

Though alchemy and numerology—two Renaissance sciences that occupied John Dee the most—are not considered sciences in a modern context, Dee did a great deal of mathematical work in both studies. In an age where numerology was perfectly well-accepted as a scientific pursuit, Dee's contemporaries considered him a top mathematician and great mind.

Dee fell out of favor with Elizabeth's successor, James VI of Scotland, and spent his senior years trying to communicate with spirits and learn the secret language of the universe.

> There is (gentle reader) nothing (the works of God only set apart) which so much beautifies and adorns the soul and mind of man as does knowledge of the good arts and sciences.

Dee was buried at Mortlake where he lived outside of London, but his grave has become lost to the world. Some of his mathematical books are on display at the Royal College of Physicians in London.

As John Dee advised Queen Elizabeth I of England, Catherine de' Medici found her own solace in the nearly constant presence of her own seer, the French physician Michel de Nostredame, more commonly known as Nostradamus today. Though his family was originally Jewish, they converted to Catholicism under the strict pressure from the Church, and Nostradamus found himself an eager student of various spiritual and physical studies. He entered the University of Avignon for medical studies at the age of 14 and later attended the University of Montpellier in hopes of earning his doctorate. The latter school expelled him when it was discovered that he was working as an apothecary. Working a trade was considered far below the class of person who should attend a university, perhaps because professors wanted their students to be able to commit every ounce of energy to their studies. From the view of the Late Middle Ages wealthy class, middle- and lower-class people with hands-on jobs were not only potentially poor students but possibly even genetically unfit to learn the higher humanities. He continued with his education via books and interviews with professionals, working hard to make a name for himself.

When the plague swept through France in the 1530s, claiming the lives of Nostradamus' wife and children, he dedicated himself to working alongside physicians to try to heal the sick and eradicate the disease from Europe altogether. His popular rose pill was developed as a prevention for the continent's biggest infectious killer, and his cure rate was among the highest of his profession. Derived from rose hips, the pill's contents supplied patients with high levels of vitamin C. Vitamin supplements, plus Nostradamus' belief in fresh air and hygiene for the sick and healthy alike, could indeed have had a positive statistical effect on the bacterial infection that was the plague.

Nostradamus' almanac, written for the year 1550, gained him widespread fame and respect as a natural philosopher and seer by his peers and royal patrons, most significantly the queen of France. Catherine de' Medici, born of Florence's notorious ruling family, had a reputation as a conjurer. With the queen's support, Nostradamus wrote his most famous book, *Les Propheties*, in 1555. The pages contained multiple predictions based on his meditations over a bowl of water and a dark mirror. He told patrons that such meditations sent him into a trance that was characterized by strong visual hallucinations of future events. He documented these visions and interpreted them as specific events that would transpire over the course of the next 2,000 years.

Of course, the Inquisition was a dangerous and omnipresent threat, even outside of Spain. Having already come to the attention of the Church by way of his predictions and calculations, Nostradamus decided to write *Les Propheties* in a coded form, whereby predictions were broken into four-line poems that used multiple languages. It was not the enormous success he perhaps hoped it would be, but nevertheless, the book was popular enough to sustain the seer and keep the book in print until modern times. Enduring through the centuries, Nostradamus' book has been interpreted to have predicted the French Revolution, the terrorist attacks on the United States of America on September 11, 2001, the bombing of Hiroshima, Japan, the death of British Princess Diana, the NASA Challenger disaster, and much more.

Nostradamus and his patroness believed wholeheartedly in his prophetic visions, while modern science—a profession in which the seer considered himself to practice—refers to his fulfilled prophecies as postdiction. Postdiction describes the method of matching so-called prophetic writing and proclamation to significant events once the events have already taken place.

Indeed, the physician and writer did not call himself a prophet, writing the following about the label:

> If I have eschewed the word prophet, I do not wish to attribute to myself such lofty title at the present time, for whoever is called a prophet now was once called a seer; since a prophet, my son, is properly speaking one who sees distant things through a natural knowledge of all creatures. And it can happen that the prophet bringing about the perfect light of prophecy may make manifest things both human and divine, because this cannot be done otherwise, given that the effects of predicting the future extend far off into time.

> Perfect knowledge of such things cannot be acquired without divine inspiration, given that all prophetic inspiration derives its initial origin from God Almighty, then from chance and nature. Since all these portents are produced impartially, prophecy comes to pass partly as predicted. For understanding created by the intellect cannot be acquired by means of the occult, only by the aid of the zodiac, bringing forth that small flame by whose light part of the future may be discerned. We need god to prosper those without him will not.

At court, Michel de Nostradame found a permanent place as a physician to the royal family. When pressured to provide specific predictions as related to the royals, he said that King Henry II would die from a wound in his eye. In 1559, while jousting at the celebration of his daughter's marriage to King Phillip II of Spain, Henry was struck in the eye by his opponent's lance. The king died ten days later.

Nostradamus died in 1566, one day after writing his will and advising his servant that he would not be alive to see the sunrise. His reputation remains that of one of the premier fortune-tellers of the Renaissance and of all time.

Chapter 23 – The Medical Renaissance

One of the most exciting facets of the European Renaissance was the physiological advances made by researchers and scientists of the day. As part of the in-vogue neoclassical education of the time, scholars studied the Greek and Latin works of ancient physicians such as Galen and Hippocrates. The ideas set forth by such great classical thinkers resonated in a compelling way with many students in 14th-century Florence and eventually the rest of the educated continent. Ambroise Pare, Leonardo da Vinci, and William Harvey, among others, conducted studies that revolutionized how sickness is understood and treated.

Claudius Galenus, more commonly known as Claudius Galen, was a 2nd-century Greek doctor who had treated the Roman emperor successfully and therefore became very famous. Since dissecting human beings was forbidden for religious reasons in his day, Galen learned how bodies worked by dissecting animals and trying to relate them to the human anatomy. His works were some of the main textbooks in medical schools throughout the Middle Ages and into the Renaissance, with anatomical observations that were fairly accurate.

In the Middle Ages, dissection and autopsies were still very rare and often considered ungodly by everyone from clerics to common peasants. The practice being out of vogue meant that physicians had precious little knowledge of the human body with which to attempt to heal it. The Greeks and Romans themselves participated very little in such procedures, but nevertheless, Renaissance students and practitioners became too curious to keep the mysteries of the inner body hidden.

In Italy, there were city appointees in charge of performing autopsies on potential murder victims, but the practice didn't become widespread until the 15th century. At that point, wealthy patients began to pay in advance for an autopsy from their physician, sometimes in hopes that it would prevent other family members from succumbing to the same illness. In many cases, doctors only investigated the skull and brain to try to determine the cause of death. The skulls of many members of the Medici family bear marks to show such analysis.

Leonardo da Vinci was particularly interested in internal medicine and the answers that could be found beneath the skin of a cadaver. Specifically, he wanted to find the link between vision, the brain, and the soul. He believed that the human soul was a very real thing and that it existed within the confines of the brain. To facilitate his research, the renowned master of fine arts personally dissected the bodies of thirty dead people. He sketched what he found within the bodies carefully, isolating muscles, nerves, and even fetal remains in three-dimensional detail. Da Vinci also experimented with frogs, noting how the amphibians died each time he broke a particular part of their spines.

In France, the surgeon Ambroise Pare experimented with considerably better intentions on his human patients, stitching together ruptured veins and arteries with delicate silk threads. As excellent a grasp of the physicality of blood vessels as Pare had, his surgeries were usually unsuccessful because of infections. That didn't stop him from learning how to restrict blood flow in individual veins by using a thread or wire in a procedure known as ligature.

Pare's battlefield medical administrations were much more fruitful and showed an innate understanding of the scientific method. When treating the wounded after a bloody battle for the Castle Villaine, Pare used the accepted method of applying boiling oil to gunshot wounds to cauterize them and destroy the poison believed to fester within. At length, the physician ran out of oil and was forced to treat the remaining troops with an ancient poultice recipe of egg yolk, rose oil, and turpentine. Unwittingly, he had stumbled upon the ideal experimental testing situation.

Pare is quoted by Leon Gordis in *Epidemiology:*

> That night I could not sleep at my ease, fearing that by lack of cauterisation I would find the wounded upon which I had not used the said oil dead from the poison. I raised myself very early to visit them, when beyond my hope I found those to whom I had applied the digestive medicament feeling but little pain, their wounds neither swollen nor inflamed, and having slept through the night. The others to whom I had applied the boiling oil were feverish, with much pain and swelling about their wounds. Then I determined never again to burn thus so cruelly the poor wounded by arquebuses.

Back in Italy, a man named Girolamo Fabrizio received his doctorate of medicine in 1559 from the University of Padua and went on to teach anatomy and surgery. As a teacher, Fabrizio radically modernized the doctoral classroom when he made classroom animal dissection a routine part of the curriculum. Through the careful opening of animal bodies, Fabrizio and his students learned the inner structures of the circulatory and digestive systems, as well as the eye and ear. The subjects that most fascinated him were the membranes he found inside of veins and developing fetuses.

Fabrizio also closely examined and anatomized the brain and throat, and in terms of the latter, he made careful hypothetical notes on how a tracheotomy might be achieved. His method included the use of vertical incision and a tracheal tube with support structures to stop it from falling into the lungs or stomach. Comparatively, Fabrizio's ideas closely match the modern surgical procedure.

An English student of Fabrizio, William Harvey picked up where his teacher had left off with concern to the blood's circulatory system. Harvey's research helped him write in detail about how the heart pumps blood to the brain and body parts, leading him to discover that blood always must flow and in one direction only. After obtaining his doctoral degree from the University of Padua, Harvey became the head doctor at St. Bartholomew's Hospital back in England. In 1615, Harvey was appointed as a Lumleian lecturer, a role in which he traveled throughout England discussing modern medicine to enlighten the kingdom. His book, *An Anatomical Disquisition on the Motion of the Heart and Blood in Animals*, explains how the heart acts as a muscular pump, moving blood first in then out of its chambers.

> The heart of animals is the foundation of their life, the sovereign of everything within them, the sun of their microcosm, that upon which all growth depends, from which all power proceeds.

An incredibly well-respected doctor of his day, Harvey became Physician Extraordinary to King James I of England, successor to Queen Elizabeth I, in 1618. As the most esteemed physician in the kingdom, Harvey was called upon to examine the bodies of four women accused of witchcraft in 1634. A blatant skeptic, Harvey's testimony saved all the defendants from conviction. It was an ironic turn of events since a Spanish physician by the name Michael Servetus had been burned at the stake in 1553 for publishing cardiovascular findings—similar to that of Harvey's—that offended the Catholic Church.

Most copies of Servetus' book, *Christianismi Restitutio*, were burned, but three copies have survived. 350 years after his execution in Switzerland, a statue of Servetus was built to commemorate him in Geneva. His was not the only brilliant mind of the Renaissance to be silenced by the Catholic Church. In the end, it might only have been the sheer multitude of forward-thinking scientists like Servetus, Howard, Pare, and da Vinci that allowed their combined knowledge to survive the wrath of the Church and its Inquisition.

Chapter 24 – The Persecuted Intellectuals

The Renaissance has an almost fairytale reputation as a magical time in Europe when literature, intellect, and scientific discovery ruled. Unfortunately, the truth is that every discovery, every medical advancement, and every mathematical equation was hard-won by a determined individual who was lucky enough to find him or herself in an environment supportive enough to not dismiss the idea outright or cry "Heresy!" and start readying the torture devices. For every successful scientist, religious reformer, and humanist writer of the period, there were more unlucky thinkers out there who suffered the unjust consequences that came of being ahead of one's time or simply in front of the wrong audience.

One of these was Giordano Bruno, born in the Kingdom of Naples in 1548. A brilliant astronomer, Bruno extended the model of the universe proposed by Nicolaus Copernicus to propose that not only did the Earth circle the sun but that other stars in the sky were suns with orbiting planets of their own. Further, Bruno believed that the universe itself had no measurable size and instead was infinite. He concluded, therefore, that the universe had no center of which to speak. The scientist's ideas not only provoked clerics still upset at the suggestion that the Earth was not the center of God's universe, but it further insinuated that there was no single "god" entity, nor heaven or hell. Furthermore, when questioned, Bruno refused to cow to the Catholic belief that bread and wine, when offered in Holy Communion, turned into the spirit and body of Jesus Christ.

After decades of traveling between France, Germany, Austria, England, and other parts of the continent, Bruno was arrested by the Venetian Inquisition and afterward sent to Rome for his trial. His arrest was based on the complaints from the parent of his tutoring student who cited the plurality of worlds theory—or the belief that there are many more suns and planets in the universe than our own—as the reason. For seven years, Giordano Bruno was held in prison while his trial went on and on. Though Bruno did try to save himself by claiming he accepted the teachings of the Church, he ultimately refused to sign a statement that recanted his scientific philosophies.

Pope Clement VIII himself declared the man a heretic and sentenced him to be executed. Bruno was hung upside down naked in a Roman square before being burned at the stake. His ashes were dumped into the Tiber River and all his books placed on a list of prohibited works.

Another Italian physicist by the name of Lucilio Vanini struggled alongside Bruno to defend his lack of religious faith in the latter 16th century. After spending his youth in the study of theology and philosophy at Naples, Vanini decided to further pursue the study of natural sciences. His curiosity and unprecedented ideas caused him to travel across Europe, supporting himself by teaching along the way.

Vanini may have been an atheist, which was itself considered heresy, but it seems more likely as evidenced by his writings that he was more of an agnostic. Regardless of his true feelings about the

Church, Vanini felt compelled to write a book that attacked atheism altogether. Most contemporaries and modern scholars agree that the book was a mere tool to remove the pressures from the Inquisition. It worked but not for long. When Vanini revealed his scientific theories, he was right back under the target of the Church. He claimed that the universe was a physical place governed by the same laws as Earth, and theorized that humans and great apes must have a common ancestor—proposing the latter theory long before Charles Darwin was even born. It was beyond blasphemous in the eyes of the Church, and in 1619, Vanini was found guilty of atheism and blasphemy by the Parliament of Toulouse. The man had his tongue cut out before he was strangled to death and burned.

Over half a century later in Poland, Kazimierz Łyszczyński was also accused of atheism, but he most certainly did subscribe to this worldview. Ironically, Łyszczyński studied for eight years under the Jesuit order of Catholics before taking a job as judge against them in estate cases. Convinced that religion was nothing but manmade dogma, the philosopher researched the subject heavily and passionately began writing his treatise, *De non existentia Dei*—or, *On the Nonexistence of God*.

The project was a secret, but an argument over repayment of a debt make Łyszczyński an enemy of an acquaintance who had seen some of his writings. Specifically, the author had scribbled "Therefore God does not exist" in the pages of a research source called *Theologia Naturalis* that tried to prove the existence of God. The book was turned in to Catholic authorities, as well as handwritten pages of Łyszczyński's own work. The accusations had their desired effect: Łyszczyński was found guilty of atheism and blasphemy and condemned to have his tongue pulled out with a hot iron before being burned alive.

Within the pages of Łyszczyński's unfinished masterwork, it reads:

Man is the creator of God, and God is a concept and creation of Man.

Chapter 25 – In the Years Following the Renaissance

During the end of the 17th century, that remarkable period of classical style education, art, and science reached a brilliant peak that culminated in the next significant era of European history: the Enlightenment. Also known as the Age of Reason, the 18th century was throughout all Europe a time in which those humanistic theories and scientific discoveries of the Renaissance were brought to the forefront and celebrated as triumphs. No longer could the Church wave its hand and order death upon the great thinkers of the continent, and no more did the people bow subserviently to an unquestioned ruler or government.

In 1789, this revolution came to a head in Paris when the self-declared National Assembly overthrew the Ancient Regime of France and ushered in the republican era. The French Revolution reverberated all the way across the Atlantic and into the heart of the French colonies, who cheered on their fellow citizens and rebelled against the slavery and exploitation of their wealthy masters and lords. That rebellion shook the foundations of North American slavery and eventually caused the abolition of slavery altogether in Europe and the Americas.

Many of the poor souls who were so persecuted and tortured under the Inquisition for their scientific, religious, or philosophical ideas were honored in the years following the Renaissance. The middle finger of Galileo Galilei 's right hand, for example, is on display at the Museo Galileo in Florence, Italy. An art sculpture dedicated to Giordano Bruno was erected at Potsdamer Platz in Berlin, Germany to commemorate his gruesome murder, and many of the other scientists condemned for being ahead of their time are memorialized in the pages of school textbooks the world over.

The intellectual growth enjoyed by all of Europe during the Renaissance was celebrated and used as the basis for an entirely new scientific industry during the Enlightenment. Thanks to those first magnified images of the moon, planets, and stars, and each early theory on gravity and objects in motion, new generations of scientific minds like Isaac Newton and Giuseppe Rosati could pick up where their predecessors left off. The work of each and every explorer, physician, astronomer, anatomist, painter, and architect moved the practice forward immeasurably until eventually we were blessed with modern medicine, artistic realism, multiple sciences, and a knowledge of the universe that runs so deep it is almost unfathomable.

Isaac Newton, having fully realized many of the physical laws that Galileo theorized, perhaps put it best:

If I have seen further, it is only because I have been standing on the shoulders of giants.

References

Cervantes. *Don Quixote de la Mancha.* 1605.

De Lille, Alain. *Liber Parabolarum,* 1175.

De Pizan, Christine. *The Book of the City of Ladies.* 1405.

Dee, John. Found in Gareth Southwell's *Words of Wisdom,* 2011.

Galilei, Galileo. A letter to the Grand Duchess Christina, 1614. Contained in Jackson J. Spielvogel's *Western Civilization: 1300 – 1815.* 2014.

Harvey, William. *An Anatomical Disquisition on the Motion of the Heart and Blood in Animals.* 1628.

Luther, Martin. *Large Catechism.* (Translation by Robert E. Smith) 1529.

Łyszczyński, Kazimierz. *De non existentia Dei,* 1674.

Malory, Thomas. *Le Morte d'Arthur: The Book of King Arthur and of His Noble Knights of the Round Table.* 1485.

Montaigne, Michel. *Of the Education of Children.* 1575.

Newton, Isaac in a letter to Robert Hooke, 1675.

Nostradamus, Michel. *The Compleat Works of Nostradamus*. Compiled by Archaneum, 2003.

Pare, Ambroise. As quoted by Leon Gordis in *Epidemiology,* 2013.

Petrarch, Francisco. As quoted in *Notable Thoughts About Women: A Literary Mosaic* by Maturin Murray Ballou, 1882.

Routh, C. R. N. *They Saw It Happen: An Anthology of Eyewitness' Accounts of Events in European History, 1450-1600*. 1965.

Shakespeare, William. *Hamlet.* 1599.

Van Norman, Louis E. *Poland: The Knight Among Nations.* 1907.

Free Bonus from Captivating History (Available for a Limited time)

Hi History Lovers!

Now you have a chance to join our exclusive history list so you can get your first history ebook for free as well as discounts and a potential to get more history books for free! Simply visit the link below to join.

Captivatinghistory.com/ebook

Also, make sure to follow us on Facebook, Twitter and Youtube by searching for Captivating History.

Check out another book by Captivating History

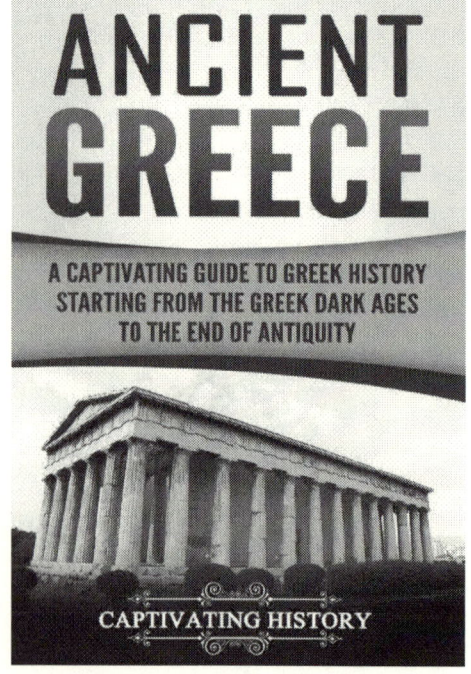

Made in United States
Troutdale, OR
10/21/2024

24004597R10075